Done

Teen Love, Teen Marriage

Teen Love, Teen Marriage

by

RUTH L. BUTCHER   MARION O. ROBINSON
ALGERNON D. BLACK   PAUL H. LANDIS
RALPH G. ECKERT   LESTER A. KIRKENDALL

EDITED BY

JULES SALTMAN

for The Public Affairs Committee

GROSSET & DUNLAP
PUBLISHERS   NEW YORK

Something To Think About

Boy AND GIRL TOGETHER—the source of much joy, and also much trouble! Oh, yes, it's wonderful. And you think it's LOVE. That's especially wonderful.

But are you sure?

When you're a teen and having fun and thrills, it's hard to stop and think about all the problems that might be involved. (It's even harder when you're a teen and *not* having fun.) Your bubbling emotions get in the way. But you do have to consider things. For instance:

Your Parent-Type Parents. Mothers and fathers certainly do have a way of getting into the picture and making it complicated. All the same, you have to get along with them. And it even may be that they are right about certain things. How do you work it out with them?

The Slippery Pink Cloud. When that delightful pink cloud called "Love" comes along and offers you a ride it is sometimes hard to tell whether it is

5

really there or you see it only because you want to
so much. And even after you get on board, it's very
easy to slip off. How do you pick the one that is
real and will last?

The "Too-Young" Roadblock. This is going to
come up, sure as anything. To some grown-ups,
everyone under the age of thirty is too young for
marriage. But it is more and more often really a
question, because the stars at the wedding—and those
who want to be stars—are getting younger every day.

The Body-to-Body Land Mine. That means SEX,
of course. It *is* a land mine, as many a young girl
and boy have discovered. Handling it without having
it explode in your face is quite a trick. Maybe you
can use some hints.

The "Wrong Religion" Drag. With people moving
around as easily as they do now (cars are getting
ever more popular and airplane rides less expensive)
the chance that you will meet and love someone of
a different religion (or even a different nationality
or race) is mighty good. Can you handle it?

There's a fresh and sensible way to look at all these
questions. A way that takes into account things as
they really are, here and now. Not as they were in
your grandmother's day. Or even in your mother's.

In the pages that follow, we have tried to gather
a special group of people. They're all grown-ups, of
course. (What else could we do?) But they are particularly smart and clear-eyed grown-ups. And, with
long experience and much talking with teenagers,

they have learned to look at matters from the teen-ager's point of view. Count on it, they can give you the fresh and sensible look at your problems that you want.

The thoughts and suggestions of these people have been gathered from the pages of Public Affairs Pamphlets, a series of publications on many important personal and social subjects that has been published for over thirty years. A list of the pamphlets involved, all copyrighted by Public Affairs Committee, Inc., and something about their authors follow:

"Coming of Age: Problems of Teen-Agers," Public Affairs Pamphlet No. 234. By Paul H. Landis, Professor of Sociology at Washington State University and author of a number of books for and about young people.

"So You Think It's Love!", Public Affairs Pamphlet No. 161. By Ralph G. Eckert, formerly head of the Department of Family Development at the University of Connecticut and now Director of Counseling and Guidance for the schools of Riverside County, California.

"Too Young to Marry?", Public Affairs Pamphlet No. 236. By Lester A. Kirkendall, Professor of Family Life at Oregon State University, author of many books on sex for young people and an outstanding leader in the field. He is a co-founder of the Sex Information and Education Council.

"If I Marry Outside My Religion," Public Affairs Pamphlet No. 204. By Algernon D. Black, Leader of the Ethical Societies in America, and teacher, writer, and radio broadcaster on subjects of social interest.

"Sex and Our Society," Public Affairs Pamphlet No. 366. By Lester A. Kirkendall with Elizabeth Ogg. Miss Ogg is a well-known free-lance writer.

For their help in bringing to you a little book that may be of great interest—and may even open up a few ideas that you had not thought about before—these authors and the Public Affairs Committee, Inc., have the editor's sincere thanks.

Jules Saltman

Contents

9

*Teen Love,
Teen Marriage*

CHAPTER 1

The Bumpy Road to Teenhood

By PAUL H. LANDIS

ALL OF US, as we begin to move from childhood to adulthood, feel a certain amount of awkwardness, doubt, and uncertainty. We want the strength, privileges and responsibilities of adults but we feel a little uncertain about how ready we are.

Not only must a teenager adjust to the rapid changes in his body that he experiences during this period. The social adjustments of adolescence, although less obvious, may be even more challenging and disturbing.

Certainly social questions cause most young people considerable concern and many anxious moments. Now begins that boy-girl problem that every person since the beginning of history has had to solve or have solved for him.

In many parts of the world parents or other relatives still assume this responsibility by finding mates for their sons and daughters. Here in our country,

From "Coming of Age: Problems of Teen-Agers," Public Affairs Pamphlet No. 234

each young person is expected to make his own selection of a marriage partner. Dating, going steady, "how to act right" on a date, become important problems—for just a few years ahead comes marriage, one of the most important ventures of adulthood.

Now begin, too, serious thoughts about plans for making a living. With new interests, the need for spending money makes a job seem important right now. There are new and attractive clothes to be acquired. Soon the boy will want a car and the girl the latest fad in jewelry.

For many of us, the most serious of new concerns are those relating to morals and "right" conduct. Religion comes in here, too. Parents tell us the answers during childhood. That makes it easy. But in adolescence we begin to spend less time in the company of parents and more time with the teenage group.

Parents are no longer there to answer our questions or to tell us what we should do. There are more and more situations where we must decide for ourselves.

This is adolescence. It is a time of growing up, a launching platform, a take-off from childhood to adulthood. It is one of the most absorbing and important periods in life. So much has to be decided and so much depends upon the decisions made.

Common Problems

The comforting thing is that most adolescents feel their worries in very much the same ways, even though they often try to pretend that they don't have a care in the world. There is always this about problems of adolescence: No matter how serious they are, you do outgrow them. Time is on the side of the adolescent, and you can't hold it back.

As a teacher, I have collected more than a thousand autobiographies of students during their later teen years. In them the young people trace their personality development. One of the most prominent features of these self-discussions by students is their description of the feelings and fears of their early teen years. I think you will be surprised at how much like your own these anxieties and fears are.

Here are the problems most often mentioned by these young people in their autobiographies:

Inferiority feelings top the list. The experience and problems described suggest that many young people just don't feel capable of meeting life. Many are concerned about the various ways in which they try to compensate for these feelings. The bravado commonly used in trying to overcome "inferiority feelings" often gets them into embarrassing situations.

Daydreaming came next. This is particularly a way girls have of trying to build a world more attractive in fancy than the one they actually live in. Boys at this stage are far more interested in things outside themselves than are girls.

Sex problems of many kinds plague youth during this period. With boys, sex problems may center about trying to control desires and fears regarding masturbation. With girls, they more often center about such problems as how to behave on a date, "going too far," and how much physical contact should be permitted to a boy.

Anxieties about temperamental traits begin in earnest in the teen years. "My temper," "my bad disposition," "my moodiness" become major concerns. An adult, even a very young adult, is not permitted the frank expression of feelings we take for granted in a child.

Many young persons worry about "introversion"— living *within* themselves too much. They are anxious when meeting new people, don't know how to talk to others, don't "feel at home" with others, or are anxious about their "manners" in more formal social situations.

Religion becomes a major concern now. And it is during adolescence that social service begins to challenge the imagination of young people. They begin to want to *do* something to improve the world. They debate questions of God, heaven and hell, the after life, and the *reason* for human existence. Why were human beings put on earth, they ask? They debate social questions, too, such as the matter of civil rights for all Americans. All these doubts and questions seem to demand quick answers. Yet, as a matter of fact, some of them will require a lifetime of thinking.

Next in the list of big problems is *breaking away from dependence upon parents.* One of the most frequent phrases of the adolescent girl of this age is "Oh, you wouldn't understand," when her mother asks questions or expresses concern about adolescent behavior. The boy is certain that his father has suddenly become an old fogy who has lost touch with things. It is during this period that he begins to refer to his father as the "old man."

The truth of the matter is, the adolescent demands new freedom to learn about life and all of a sudden wants to put the restrictions of childhood behind him.

This adolescent transition may cause a lot of anxiety both to the adolescent and to his parents. This is a time when young people become a little disillusioned about parents and adults in general. They chafe at adult demands imposed upon them. The opinions of those their own age are often valued much higher than those of parents and teachers.

Your Family and You

Very often during adolescence parents seem to stand like a great barrier to freedom. They stand for all the helplessness of a small child that the burgeoning teenager is fighting to overcome.

In part, this may be true. But there are some things young people don't understand about their position. In some ways they want to be grown-up; in others, they don't. Parents may not always know just how to act in some situations. They are never quite sure how grown-up their offspring feels at a particular time.

There's no denying that parents are sometimes downright unreasonable. They require a lot of tolerance on the part of an adolescent. Then there are some issues on which parents and teenagers naturally don't always see eye-to-eye.

These areas of teenage disagreement with parents have been given a lot of study. The really big issues seem to revolve about "spending money," "outside activities and social life" (one of the big conflicts of social life is "getting in at night," or curfew), "sharing the work," "doing school work conscientiously," "clothes," and "use of the family car."

This last one is a particularly hot issue between boys and their parents. The girl is not quite so demanding about the use of the family car as is her brother. It's her date's responsibility to provide the transportation. Her real problem is parental objection to going out in the boy friend's car at night.

These problems come up in hundreds of different ways in the relationships between parents and growing teenagers. They are normal. They are characteristic of parent-child relationships in our society. There is no easy answer. Parents and teenagers have to be reasonable people, and have to try to discuss and work out their points of disagreement and areas of friction.

The essence of this problem is that neither the adolescent nor his parent is sure of how far it is safe for the adolescent to go undirected. A few successes in adult situations may make a young person heady with self-confidence and irritable of any restraints. A few failures may make the parent reluctant to grant further freedom or may weaken his belief that his adolescent is ready for freedom.

Junior may have been able to perform a grown-up role during an entire summer when he was out working on a farm. But this does not necessarily mean that he is mature enough to drive to a nearby city for a Saturday night of fun with three pals. While Junior may consider these situations as similar, his parents recognize that when a young boy is out with his pals in a car there are four boys to reckon with rather than one.

The fact that Martha made a botch of her first date—was noisy and bold, or shy and awkward—may suggest a heart-to-heart talk and a few rules, but it should not destroy her parents' belief in her readiness to begin dating.

(If parents remember two rules—"Be slow to criticize." "Be quick to sympathize."—the chances are that they will continue to receive the confidences and questions of their adolescent youngsters and remain in a position to offer help.)

(It helps young people to remember that though Dad and Mom lived in a different day, they once faced most of these problems, too.)

If one trusts them and tries to cooperate, parents can be a real help more often than a hindrance. It is when adolescents act too immature for their age that mature status is denied them. (It is up to each teenager to demonstrate his adult status, not just demand it.)

Parents Are People

It is not unusual at this period for the teenager to develop a little hostility toward one or both of his parents, particularly if he or she has been held down too closely.

In a good many instances the hostility young people show could be greatly reduced by a few honest words and a little clear thinking on both sides. For example, take this situation:

"No, Bill," Dad says, "No movie for you tonight!"

"But why?"

Eager to get back to his newspaper, Dad doesn't bother to remind Bill of their agreement that, until his grades improve, he'll limit himself to one movie a week. Instead, Dad just repeats:

"No, I said! No movie tonight!"

This approach reminds Bill of all the power his Dad exercises over his life. Suddenly Dad seems like a tyrant and Bill is likely to let loose a flood of hostility about "never any freedom," "always cooped up," "treated like a prisoner." Then the words may fly or the silence may pile up like a hostile wall between them.

With each repetition of this kind of situation, their relationship grows worse. Honesty and concern for the opinions and happiness of one another is gradually crowded out by increasing resentment—on Bill's part, resentment of arbitrary authority; on Dad's part, resentment of impertinence and rebellion.

The same situation handled with an honest regard for the facts would leave father and son feeling closer together rather than farther apart.

Both parent and son or daughter need to remember that by the time a young person reaches adolescence he is capable of a good deal of adult reasoning. Parents owe him a sound and reasonable explanation for the rules and demands they make. The young person, in turn, must get in the habit of thinking in terms of his own general health and welfare, not just fun.) A boy or girl of twelve or fourteen years of age is fully capable of realizing and accepting the fact that passing an English exam, for example, is far more important than "taking in a show" with the crowd.

The "pleasure principle" rules the young child's life. Whatever is pleasant at the moment is vastly more important to him than any future gain. By adolescence, experience has proved that a little self-denial or hard work often pays off in far greater satisfaction in the future.

Recognizing this reasoning ability, appealing to good sense instead of demanding blind obedience, listening to one another's opinions or arguments on an issue, will do much to build a strong bond of companionship between the generations. Hostility does not grow in soil rich in respect.

(Those parents who feel that their adolescents are lacking in the respect and the honor they deserve should remind themselves, too, that a certain amount of rebellion is nothing more than a symptom of coming adulthood. For this reason, parents must be tolerant of a little hostility. Later, these hostilities will vanish and young people will become understanding equals.)

The story of the parent and adolescent being so close and understanding that the adolescent always runs to mama and papa with an important problem is probably fiction. In a study of over 5,500 high school seniors made by the State College of Washington it was found that only about one in ten boys *always* talked over personal problems with a parent, and scarcely one of five girls did. About half of the boys and girls stated that they *occasionally* took their problems to their parents. More than one in four said they *seldom* or *never* discussed their problems with parents.

From the time the adolescent begins to hang on the telephone talking by the hour with bosom companions with whom he or she has just spent all day, the parent must recognize that the offspring has found more understanding ears among his or her own generation than in the adult generation.

Steps Toward Independence

It is characteristic of young people to waver back and forth in their quest for independence. Although they suddenly want and feel a need for the status of independent adults, they continue to depend on parents. What parents and adolescents alike often fail to understand is that the nature of their need for parents has changed.

 (Young people need their mothers and fathers more in a "stand by" capacity than as confidants.) Like beginning swimmers with more courage than experience, they don't want help. They want to know that someone is ready to step in and help if called upon.

And when they do call for help, they want help, not lectures, sermons, or "I told you so."

This new sense of independence of the adolescent, which puts the parent in the background, is difficult for many parents to accept. "Johnny used to tell us everything," Mama says to Dad, and feels a little hurt and left out now that Johnny wants her advice only when he is in trouble.

A ten-year-old boy generally tells his parents about a classroom or playground incident, a fight, or a misunderstanding. At fifteen, the same boy is more likely to try to work everything out by himself or with a pal's help, and to consult Mom and Dad only when things go from bad to worse.

Love, too, changes rather strangely during this time. Adolescents often resent physical displays—hugs or kisses from Mom and Dad. They feel uncomfortable if called by the familiar pet name in the presence of their friends. But this does not mean they don't want or need their parent's love.

Trust, confidence, and encouragement replace the hugs and kisses parents use in order to show love to a younger child. The adolescent in turn shows his love and confidence by seeking advice on important matters and by having pet names for his parents and family.

One college girl recalled with great tenderness the special way her parents chose to show their love and sympathy for a growing-up daughter: "I used to be amazed by the way some of my friends treated their parents and were treated by them. It seemed as if their mothers were always whining or barking at them, finding fault, suspecting things, being disgusted with them when they acted childish and tomboyish, but refusing to treat them like adults. Most of these friends avoided their parents like the plague. Parents were people who made unreasonable demands, uninteresting plans, and unworkable rules.

"My own parents must have been more special than I realized. I remember Mother making me feel very grown up by lending me her beaver coat for a football game, borrowing a pair of my own earrings when she and Daddy went out, and asking my advice about refurnishing a room. Both of them talked to me very much as they talked to one another. They respected my privacy and didn't try to force themselves into my special interests.

"But when something went wrong at school or in our club—when I felt all mixed up or childish and unsure of myself—they never insisted that I 'snap out of it and act your age' as some parents do. They were more likely to suggest things we might all do together. In this way they were my special friends until, after a while, I'd begin to long to be back with the gang again. When that time came, they were always happy to let me go."

Sisters and Brothers

Then there are the brothers and sisters you have to deal with. Some of us have lived all our lives in the shadow of the praise and acclaim given to a beautiful sister or an extremely bright brother. In adolescence we begin to express resentment at being overshadowed. We begin to declare our independence from brothers and sisters.

These are often hard adjustments to make, and it is not always easy to overcome inferiority feelings built by having to take second place in the family. Here is Chuck's account of a big brother:

"My brother was three years ahead of me in school and a very brilliant student. My parents, as well as all the teachers, expected me to match his record of good grades. I guess I was well hidden when the brains were passed out. While my brother got A's with very little effort, I slaved for C's.

"The more I heard about my brilliant brother, the more inadequate I felt. To keep from displaying my feelings, I spent no more time with my family than was absolutely necessary. Instead of staying at home evenings with my brother and sisters, I would go to the homes of my friends where I wasn't constantly hounded by the subject of grades."

When Chuck wrote this account, he was in a college several hundred miles from the one his older brother was attending. He no longer had to live under the shadow of his brother's record and was beginning to feel as though he could be satisfied with the achievements of which he was capable.

There are both good things and bad things about having brothers and sisters. A sociologist has written about this experience in the life of adults. She says: "Most of us, on becoming closely acquainted with men and women of apparent maturity, have found that in certain aspects of their personalities they are still much under the influence of brother or sister, still smarting under childhood patterns. It does not matter that they are now successful in their own right; they must still convince brother or sister of their success.

"One man's whole life is spent in achieving goals which his sister unconsciously set for him years ago; he must prove to her that he can do it. One woman's life is shattered because of her ambivalent attitude of hatred and love for a brother who dominated her childhood." (Jessie Bernard, *American Family Behavior*.)

There it is in a nutshell. We are never the same after a brother or sister comes into our lives. So getting away from them may be a lifelong job rather than one that can be solved in a day.

While we are in the family we must get along with them and share fairly. Soon each will grow up and establish his own family and his own way of life. In adulthood many childhood rivalries between brother and sister will evoke an understanding smile.

In spite of all its difficulties, family life with brothers and sisters is an experience that most young people will always look back upon with pleasure. Experience in the family will be our best training for getting along and meeting problems in the new family that we will establish after marriage.

CHAPTER 2

Growing Pains— The Physical Kind

By PAUL H. LANDIS

So FAR AS WE KNOW, animals behave as they feel like behaving, except when other animals affect their behavior by fighting them or dominating them or intimidating them through fear. Watching hens in a chicken pen will show, for example, that there is an established pecking order. Each hen ranks in food privileges on the basis of having outpecked the other hens. The one who outpecks them all rules the roost as well as the food trough. When it comes to matters of looks, manners, and morals, they apparently let nature take its course.

Man can never do this. Even in infancy and childhood parents begin to teach us to exercise control over our desires. In adolescence we are constantly reminded to "act our age." Parents and teachers reprimand us with, "You're too big to behave that way," or "You're a big boy now." Thus we learn that becoming an adult takes a lot of harnessing of feelings and control of fears and desires.

From "Coming of Age: Problems of Teen-Agers," Public Affairs Pamphlet No. 234

Sex presents one of the big problems of learning to live with one's self and others during adolescence. A class of boys in a large city high school were asked to write, without signing their names, about their personal problems. Almost every one indicated that he was troubled about masturbation, sex dreams, and seminal discharges.

In early adolescence the boy and girl pass through the stage of physical development called puberty. The boy's glands develop the ability to produce semen. Semen is the male sex fluid which is required for reproduction. Tension for the release of these fluids is a normal part of adolescence.

Any normal boy will have emissions of sexual fluids during "wet dreams," as the glands release themselves. Masturbation at some time during the adolescent years is also nearly universal.

This maturing of sex powers is a normal part of growth. Discharge of semen in dreams or during masturbation will not destroy one's physical health. Many fears have been built up about it because many years ago a man wrote a very unscientific treatise claiming insanity and various sicknesses were produced by such seminal discharges. Some parents believe this is so. Others unwisely use such fears in teaching young people about sex.

The emission of semen is not harmful. However, worrying about anything excessively *is* harmful. Due to many false beliefs about the effects of masturbation and nocturnal emissions, many boys spend anxious hours worrying about their behavior. The facts are that seminal discharge has no relationship to acne, nosebleed, feeblemindedness, and mental disease, nor does it affect a boy's capacity to be a father later on.

Studies show that most girls do not feel the same kinds of tensions that boys feel. They want to be coddled and loved, but sex desire as a direct tension is much less a problem. Most girls are concerned about "how far to go," for sex with them involves not only moral questions but the risk of pregnancy and disgrace.

Your Body and You

If you are an undersized boy and often tempted to bravado to show that you are as big as the rest of the boys, be careful. You probably can't offset their taunts of "peewee," "runt," "midget," or whatever nickname they have for you. It is well to remember that as the group gets a little older, physical strength and size will not be the measure of accomplishment.

What will count will be the things you can do, your mental ability and your competence.

There are some disadvantages in being an extremely small or extremely large boy or man. But these are secondary matters that in no way reflect one's social worth. A part of being grown up is the ability to recognize one's assets and shortcomings, and to learn to live with them.

Adolescent girls, too, often worry if their bodies and emotions still seem to them to be more like those of a child than of a young woman.

Actually, according to one authority, the slow-to-develop girl is "significantly higher than the early-maturing in traits related to personal appearance and attractiveness, in expressiveness and activity, in buoyancy, in poise, and cheerfulness, and also in sociability, leadership, and prestige." This author noted that such a girl's slow-to-develop body, upon finally reaching maturity, most often "tends to conform closely to our American standards of beauty of figure." (Harold E. Jones, *The Family in a Democratic Society*.)

If you are a girl who has reached puberty ahead of your class, you may feel you are in a most awkward position. Remember that in a year or two the rest will catch up.

The older boys may be wanting to date you, and you may be wanting to date while the rest of the girls you know are still playing with dolls and "hating boys." If you date, however, you run the risk of losing your girl friends and being left out of the old, familiar crowd. The older girls may not accept you because you're younger.

This is a good time to be patient and wait for the rest to catch up. However, if parents and teachers feel that you are grown-up in studies and interests, the problem may be solved by your being moved a class or two ahead where all the girls have the same interests.

If you feel you don't fit your age group in looks or growth, remember that time and nature are on your side. Soon these differences will be corrected and work themselves out.

Trips and Bumps

Most adolescents have inferiority feelings. They

find so many new people and new situations to deal with, so many decisions to be made, that many unintentional mistakes are made.

The blows during adolescence teach us, in the end, what situations to avoid and when to move ahead. The small child learns the rules of physical safety by burns, scratches, and bumps. Adolescents learn social safety in much the same way. During adolescence, however, the burns, scratches, and bumps are emotional ones.

As a result of them, during later adolescence we begin to limit our activities to those situations in which we feel confident about succeeding. We pick friends of like interests, we choose tasks that we can perform adequately.

We limit our hobbies to the things we have learned to excel in. We cut down the activities to proportions we can handle. Success in such situations brings praise and builds self-confidence. Eventually, one comes into adulthood feeling that he can both live and let live.

Ordinarily, we cannot suffer defeats without making some comeback fight. If we can't fight in the area where we have been deflated, we try another. Maybe we can't box, but we can play basketball. If we can't win at love, then we can try books.

June tells of her problems of adjustment: "I was healthy, I was tall, but I was also fat. This never bothered me at home where my family and playmates accepted it.

"Then I started to school. It was there I found I couldn't run as fast, jump rope as long, or play baseball like the other kids could. I was usually one of the last ones chosen when they picked out teams for school sports. I became aware of this as I progressed through grade school. Feeling so left out, I turned more and more to my studies.

"The thought of starting high school filled me with dread. I could almost hear the upperclassmen remarking about my size. But I decided to try athletics again and turned out for girl's basketball. Much to my surprise, because of my height I became a valuable forward on the team. Even so, it took me a long time to get over the self-consciousness I felt while on the basketball floor.

"This same self-consciousness led me to refuse dates in high school with the excuse that I was going to be an 'old maid and career woman.' I still have not overcome using this rationalization with the fellows."

At the time she wrote, there were still a few painful spots in June's personality, but she was actually a more interesting and capable person than she would have been had she not had to fight to find a place for herself.

Here is Ted's experience after the divorce of his parents. His situation is not uncommon today, yet he reacted by healthy, realistic compensation, rather than by sinking into defeat and self-pity. The divorce occurred during his first year of high school in a small rural community that had little tolerance for divorce. Ted writes:

"I needed something to make up for the loss of companionship of my father, and something to replace the satisfaction I was missing because I could not play with other children. The only way I could get this satisfaction was to excel my classmates and make them look up to me. So I began to study harder, work harder, and strive harder to fulfill this desire to excel.

"This is the reason that today I want to be the best athlete, the best student, and the most popular man. This is the reason I want to do greater things than anyone else. This goes back to the divorce of my parents with its attendant circumstances, which developed in me a self-consciousness, preventing me from associating with other people, and leaving me, as the only outlet, a strong desire to excel other people."

Don't Overdo It

We all compensate for feelings of inferiority. It's the natural way to keep from taking a complete beating and giving up. However, a few cautions about compensation are necessary.

There is always some danger of overdoing it a little. It is acceptable to specialize in those activities that we do quite well, and to emphasize our good points. But it is not acceptable to overstress our achievements to the point of "grandstanding" or "hogging the show." Everyone soon tires of a show-off and makes it a point to avoid or belittle him.

The same is true of being the "class bully" in order to compensate for low scholastic achievement. Or of overdoing the flashy clothes and lipstick in order to gain attention.

Daydreaming

Daydreaming is another way to escape from feelings of inferiority. In the magic world of make-believe, we can be the central character: the hero or the heroine, the leader, the victor, the roaring success. Through the fantasy of daydreams our every wish comes true. Here is one daydreamer:

"My name is Carol. Although I am in my late teens, I still feel like a little girl on tiptoe looking into a warm room of companionship through a cold window of loneliness. If people knew I felt that way, they would say it was impossible for a child in a family of seven to feel alone, but I can assure them that it is only too real.

"I was born on a farm in a very close-knit family group. Every Sunday I was queen of a large gathering of relatives, since I was the only small child in the group, but this high status was soon shattered as the family increased in size. When we moved from Kansas to a Western state, my real loneliness began. There we had no relatives and there were no friends. My father had a low-paying job. The family steadily increased in size. With each new arrival there was a tightening of the family budget and new responsibility was placed on me.

"For as long as I can remember, I have been given the responsibility of all my younger brothers and sisters. I have never been a child playing with them. I have always been a small and efficient overseer. My brothers and sisters soon regarded me as someone to hide from because they couldn't have fun when I was around.

"When the family went to town on Saturday, I was hardly ever allowed to go along. My parents didn't want to be bothered with all of the children, so left some behind for Carol to take care of. 'Leave Carol' is a phrase I learned to hate.

"I became indifferent to my parents and was unable to play with children my own age. I simply did not know how to get along with them. More and more I withdrew within myself. For the lack of affection of my parents and lack of association with others, I compensated in daydreams and by stroking the more sensitive parts of my body. As I grew older, I retired further and further within myself and played fascinating games in my imagination."

Carol's world was too severe for her. She created another. We can be quite sure that it was, in most respects, the opposite of the one in which she had been forced to live.

Daydreams can serve to cushion the harsh realities of life. All of us need them at times. In the end, however, we must face real-life situations and solve our problems in a real world. As we get older and have greater control over our own life, there is less need to escape to an imaginary world.

This does not mean that we will not at times need such an escape. Love stories, novels, movies, spectator sports, radio listening, and televiewing all thrive because of our need for recreational escape from the world of reality.

Getting Along with Others

The small child is self-centered. Everything revolves around him and his possessions. He seeks to satisfy his desires in the quickest and easiest way. As he grows older, he grows away from such attitudes about himself and others.

Parents have told the child what to do and what not to do in his relations with others. Theirs is the major responsibility for the early training of the young in the rules of human relations. This simplifies life for young children because it reduces the number of choices and decisions they must make during the years of inexperience.

As the child grows older, society expects him to become increasingly self-reliant and to assume greater responsibility for his own actions. Gradually he learns that in order to become accepted by others, he must respect the rights of others. Adolescence is a critical period in the development of this awareness of the rights of others.

Learning To Make Decisions

During the adolescent period of increasing self-reliance, parents recede into the background as the decision makers. More and more, the responsibility for taking a course of action falls upon one's own shoulders. This growing-up process is accelerated by the fact that as we grow older we spend more time away from home and parents.

If parents are not with us, they certainly cannot tell us what to do. They can only hope that the years of training spent in the family nest have prepared us in such a way that, once out of it, we will "fly right"— make good decisions and behave in a manner that they would approve. If they have done well we have conscience as our guide.

The conscience is really the voice of our parents, our religious leaders, our teachers, and of our own experience reminding us of the possible consequences of a contemplated course of action that is contrary to our standards. It reminds us of the ideas we have acquired about what is the right and the wrong thing to do in certain situations.

In this area of morals, ideals, and religion, here are the top issues checked by over 5,500 high school seniors in a study made by the State College of Washington:

A third of all the girls and almost as many of the boys checked "making something of myself" as their top problem. Here we see the budding of a serious sense of responsibility. The next most frequently checked item was "worry about mistakes I've made." Here is the conscience at work.

As we go on down the list we find worries about "how to do my best," "concern about religion, swearing, bad habits," "understanding the things people do," "cheating," "ideals," "morals," and "reputation."

A nationwide poll of thousands of young people by Purdue University showed that young people do not always live up to their own standards on things like smoking and drinking. We may be sure there are many pangs of conscience here, for the conscience hurts when you fail to live up to your standards.

Only half of the boys who smoke approve of it. Although fewer girls than boys smoke, girls who smoke more often approve of smoking than do boys who smoke. When it comes to drinking, most boys and girls who drink don't approve of drinking. It is pretty obvious that if a few showed a little spunk and refused to drink the gang probably wouldn't do it.

This same study showed that few of those who cheat think it is justified. Very few believe that "everyone cheats."

Sometimes little violations of behavior standards are a part of our revolt against being dictated to by adults. Sometimes parents may have been too strict too long and we feel we have to rebel to be free. Sometimes we hesitate to resist the pressure of the teenage group for fear we will be unpopular or lose friends.

Actually, one rarely loses the kind of friends he wants by standing by his principles. At the time it may not seem that this is true. In the end, our friends have greater respect for us for having the courage of our convictions.

That Old Spilt Milk

Young people in trouble should realize they are not alone; we all make a few mistakes. Our parents made them, our grandparents made them. Growing up is never sure and easy. To lick selfishness and our other faults and failings is a long battle.

As adolescents we tend to brood over past mistakes, to cry over spilt milk. Past embarrassments can haunt us and trouble us endlessly with a guilty conscience.

Even childhood deeds may come up to taunt us

during adolescence. Here is a college girl looking back on a childhood experience that to her, at the time, was mere innocent play. Later she learned that such behavior was considered "naughty." Now in late adolescence the recollection is mortifying.

"My first play group I shudder to remember. Before I even started to school, when I was only four years old, three little boys just older than I was brought us the mail every day and stayed to play. My sexual experiences began then and lasted till I was nine years old, when my mother decided it was time for me to learn the facts.

"I was horrified at what I'd done, but I didn't tell her. All the kids except me seemed to have been informed long before about such matters, and I had a very bad name.

"Immediately I changed myself completely. I wouldn't even so much as listen to a dirty story. To this day I can count on the fingers of one hand the times I've forced myself to accept a date, but I've never gone twice with the same boy."

The best way to get over a haunting mistake is to talk it over honestly and frankly with a teacher, counselor, parent, or someone in whom you have confidence. This will help you get over the shame and pain of conscience, and to start afresh.

Past mistakes need not cloud our future if we will face them honestly. We must say to ourself, "I'll chalk that one up to experience." With such an attitude, we will seldom make the same mistake again. Thus we can go ahead building our character.

And Now—Dating

No teenager can avoid the dating problem. Those who date worry about whether they should go steady, how to act on a date, and a lot of other problems. Those who don't date worry about the fact that they don't or can't date the person they prefer.

Boys worry because they are afraid to ask, and girls about the fact that the boys are afraid to ask. There are a lot of notions about this dating business.

Those who don't date have lots of company. Does that mean they never will date and never will marry? Far from it.

Bashfulness, lack of spending money, or lack of self-confidence often keep boys from dating. Half the boys in one opinion poll thought girls should be as free as boys in asking for dates, and almost a third thought it would be a good idea if girls would pay half the expenses incurred on a date. Fewer girls had the same opinion on both points. Anyway, these are some of the reasons why so many boys don't ask the girl they would like to date.

Later on, as self-confidence, allowances and income increase, these same boys will date, and more girls will have a chance to date then, too. Many very fine and serious boys and girls do not date because they do not happen to appeal to others their own age. They may be more mature and serious. Later, as the rest catch up in size and seriousness, the opportunities for dating are increased.

During this time, don't fool yourself by thinking

that good looks, fancy clothes, polished manners, and "big stuff" acting is what counts. Just learn to be yourself, and, of course, to improve yourself as you go along. Actually most young people feel a little awkward and ill at ease. A lot of this feeling leaves you as you grow older and have more social experience.

Dating Behavior

There is a lot of talk about how to behave on a date. That is one of the big worries of the girl in dating. And, of course, parents are always very anxious about how their teenage boys and girls will conduct themselves. We may as well recognize at the outset that there are no set rules.

Throughout early adolescence, a boy is expected to be somewhat more awkward socially than a girl. More likely than not he will not think of such niceties as opening doors, holding the girl's chair, and so on. By fourteen or so, if he has dated, he is expected to be able to think of "someplace to go" or "something to talk about" when with his date.

Boys are expected to act more or less the same throughout their teen years, except that they should gain a little in polish and self confidence as they grow in experience. Girls, however, play a more complex part in adolescent social life, and the girl who is unaware of the social niceties expected of her may be at a loss to understand a decrease in popularity or dates.

Harold Jones observed as a result of studies by the Institute of Child Welfare that "at the beginning of adolescence the group standard for conduct among girls emphasizes a quiet, demure, rather lady-like demeanor. By the age of fifteen this has altered, and we find that the girls who are now most popular in their sets are active, talkative, and marked by a kind of aggressive good fellowship."

In the younger ages, dating in groups avoids a lot of the problems of boy-girl relations, particularly if the group goes to school functions or to a neighborhood theatre and returns directly home. When they get to the car age, parents get more anxious. This is partly because the automobile is the great killer of the teen years, partly because they are anxious about the moral code of the crowd of young people with whom their children associate.

Parents rightly want to know whom their son or daughter is dating. They feel much safer if they know the person and something of his background and reputation. Parents feel less anxiety if the young man comes into the home and gets acquainted with the family. This is the courteous thing for young teen-daters to do.

The questions of kissing, "going steady," and the big one—sex—are common to all young people starting their dating life. Let's consider them in detail in the next chapter.

Finally, here are some rules for personality development that will also make you a more interesting person and a more interesting date.

1. *Be yourself.* This means accepting your own standards and ideals and sticking with them. No one can live by the other person's rules, unless they are

the same as his own. Stick by the things which are your honest convictions and work at improving your faults.

2. *Accept yourself for what you are.* It's all right to have heroes and to imitate people you admire. But (becoming adult requires accepting yourself for what you are as well as seeking broader horizons.) Most people aren't pretty or perfect. The most interesting people are not necessarily the best looking, or the best dressed. Everyone has good points. Emphasize them; accentuate the positive.

3. *Accept others as they are.* Don't pick on their weaknesses or humiliate them. Recognize their good points and appreciate them.

4. *Be friendly.* Friendliness wins friends. Be kind and friendly to everyone and considerate of feelings and wishes. Glum, sour people live lonely lives.

5. *Be an interesting person* by having many interests outside yourself. Your feelings and hurts, worries and petty weaknesses aren't much concern to others and will not be to you if you become an outgoing person, building new hobbies, cultivating your abilities, looking for new experiences and new friends.

6. *Make cheerfulness a habit.* One of the sourest men I ever knew became a new person when a new boss took over and told him he had to quit growling at students who came to the window where he sat taking student fees. "Be pleasant or seek another job," he was told. He stayed and became a pleasant person. Along with the improvement of his disposition came improved health.

Cheerfulness and hopefulness do much to make us

attractive both to others and to ourselves. Defeat is often of our own making. Self-pity, anxiety, and despondency are wretched companions. That is why we all tend to avoid persons who cultivate such personalities.

CHAPTER 3

The Dating Bit—And Sex

By RALPH G. ECKERT

SHOULD YOU LET a boy kiss you on your first date? Is it wise to "go steady" in high school? What's the difference between "necking" and "petting"? Can you be popular if you don't "make out"? Is it all right for an engaged couple who love each other to have sex relations before marriage? How can you know if it is really love?

These are just a few of the most common questions that today's young people are asking. Whether the students live in a lumbering town in Oregon, in Reno, Nevada, in an underprivileged section of San Francisco or Los Angeles, in Mormon Salt Lake City or rural Georgia, their questions are often the same.

Old cultural patterns are changing and new ones are growing up. But not all of the old patterns were bad nor are all the new ones good.

In the last thirty or forty years there has been a pretty steady increase in juvenile delinquency, and a

From "So You Think It's Love!", Public Affairs Pamphlet No. 161

startling increase in divorce. We must not judge from these facts, however, that society is "going to the dogs." The growth of democracy has brought with it greater freedom of choice. But freedom is not the same as happiness.

 Freedom to choose also brings freedom to choose unwisely. (Society and parents have given young people greater freedom during dating and courtship without at the same time giving them the facts needed to make intelligent choices.)

Take for example this business of dating. If you are in high school and aren't dating, you may be beginning to feel that you are different. Actually, the vast majority of students in high school do not date regularly, and probably most of them do not date at all.

Of course, you all pretend that you do. You may feel you have to because everybody else does, and the others feel they have to because you do. Wouldn't it be interesting to take a poll in your school, in which nobody had to sign his name, and ask the kids honestly to indicate how many had dated in the last month, the last week, or are dating regularly, or going steady? The results would probably surprise everyone.

A college dean recently was concerned because, as she said, "The vast majority of our students are not dating at all." So, for heaven's sakes don't feel like an "ugly duckling" just because you haven't a date.

And Going Steady

Since, if we are smart, we no longer depend on

"love at first sight" but realize (that we *grow into love*) (See next chapter), (dating and going steady become stages in the development of love feelings and intimacy, to be followed by the engagement stage and then marriage itself.)

But dating and going steady are not only important in the development of our relationship with the opposite sex. They are important in our development as people. Our (best chance for a happy marriage is to participate in a lot of group dating) (parties, picnics, church groups, etc.) during the junior high years— roughly, grades seven, eight, and nine. In senior high, group dating activity continues but couples begin to pair off and to go to and from parties with other couples, or double dating. Gradually, as you grow in self-confidence and in your ability to be a good companion, you become ready for single dating.

Patterns of Dating

There are several patterns of dating you can follow. One might be to "play the field," not going with any girl or boy more than once or twice. Or you may go out frequently with one girl and yet both of you feel free to go out with anyone else who asks you for a particular occasion.

After a lot of experience in "playing the field" and becoming good at getting and asking for dates, and having found out through this wide dating experience the type of person you really enjoy, you then begin to date a particular person more or less regularly.

When two people have gone together long enough

to know that they really enjoy each other better than anyone else, they decide to go steady. This, in effect, announces to the world that neither is interested in dating with others. After going steady for about a year, they normally grow more and more in love. Or they may come to see that they didn't really enjoy each other or the same type of activity, and break up.

This should not be thought of as a "heart-breaking" experience. The most happily married people have usually gone steady with several people and "broken up" before they found the person whom they *continued to enjoy* and came to love.

One of the difficulties now is that of getting to know other young people in large schools and large groups. All teenagers and young people should belong to some small co-ed group where group dating is natural. Otherwise, when they do get well enough acquainted to be asked, or to ask, for a date, and the date is pleasant, they are apt to rush into going steady too soon. Then they wear the sweater or pin that tells other boys and girls they are not interested in dating them.

It is probably easier that way, but do such young people get to know enough members of the other sex really to learn what kind of person they would be happiest with? Too often when they begin to tire of each other—as is the natural thing for young people who are not really mature enough to form permanent attachments—they keep on going steady, even though they don't really enjoy each other as much as they would enjoy "trying out" some new and exciting person.

Sometimes such steady-daters are afraid of hurting the other person's feelings. Sometimes they are afraid of not having any dates if they break up. They may actually be failing to learn how to make and keep new friends—may be passing up the opportunity to develop deeper understanding of the opposite sex by associating with many different types of young people. They may be getting into a rut and becoming a couple of "clinging vines" who are dependent on each other and afraid to trust their own ability to make and keep friends. They may even marry, and yet never really enjoy each other.

There is one variation of going steady that may have some merit in a large school or community where it is hard to get acquainted with people. That is, to agree to go steady for a limited period and then break up for a period, coming back together again later if desired. This makes it easy to make the break without hurt feelings.

How Fast Are You Growing?

Recent studies have indicated that *when* we develop has a great deal to do with our attitudes towards ourselves during adolescence. First of all, girls tend to develop earlier than boys. Along about eleven or twelve years of age the girls begin to outgrow the boys. Actually, between twelve and thirteen most girls are bigger and heavier and probably stronger than boys.

This is a little hard on the boys' egos. Unconsciously they resent the girls' being bigger than they are. They begin to tease them and to avoid them. The boys get together in their own gangs because they feel more comfortable there. The girls resent this behavior on the part of the boys, so they get together in their own gangs, too.

But after a year or two the boys begin this same "adolescent spurt." By fifteen they have usually caught up and passed the girls and they tend to go on growing after the girls have stopped, so that eventually they become considerably taller.

The Sex Story Today

After centuries of suppressing the physical aspects of attraction between the sexes, we have in the last few decades gone to the opposite extreme and are overemphasizing it.

Advertisers have discovered that there is nothing like "the frame of a dame" to get attention. Consequently, women in all stages of undress adorn the covers of magazines and billboards. The movies, having discovered that scantily clad females increase the box office at the theatres, have gone as far as censorship will allow (and occasionally beyond). As a result, lots of girls, trying to imitate the movie stars, have taken to sweaters and plunging necklines until boys are much more impressed by their sexuality than their femininity.

As one boy put it, "Some of these gals look as though they'd been poured into their clothes, only somebody forgot to say 'when.'" Frequently such girls don't know whether to be flattered or insulted when a boy gives them the wolf whistle.

Dancing

Sexual attraction has also been emphasized increasingly in the way we dance. Down through the ages we have had various kinds of folk dances. This type of dance calls for a great deal of physical activity but a minimum of physical contact. But since World War I we have gone in almost exclusively for ballroom dancing, in most places.

Styles in ballroom dancing change rapidly, but for a long time such a pastime for a boy or girl meant more in the way of physical contact than of activity. At one recent period, dancing seemed to mean physical contact alone, with movement at a minimum.

During that stage, a university professor expressed concern that on his campus the pattern was becoming one in which a boy danced all evening with the same girl. "Dancing is no longer sociable," he said. "They don't exchange dances, they don't even talk. They just put their arms around each other and walk around."

Of that kind of dancing, a college student said when asked why he wasn't going to a certain affair: "Frankly, I don't like dancing. To me, it's just petting to music."

The newest dances with their odd names (frug, watusi, and many more) no longer involve much physical contact. In fact, some are more like solos than they are duet dancing. But they still have a strong element of sexuality and a suggestion of abandonment. And an occasional new dance style calls for even more close contact between the two partners than in the past.

Recently a revival of folk dancing (as well as folk singing) has been taking place. You will be wise to do everything you can to encourage this development in your school and community. Like so many things that meet a real need, folk dancing has come back with a bang in many places. It is better exercise, and many young people think it's a lot more fun than ordinary ballroom dancing.

Necking

Sociologist Kimball Young once remarked that the automobile had done more to change the patterns of courtship than anything that had happened in two thousand years. What it has done is to give young people more freedom. Today you are enjoying more freedom to be alone than any group of young people has ever been allowed in our culture.

This freedom makes possible what is variously referred to as "necking," "smooching," and "making out," among other names. And it has helped to put a different value on the kiss.

One of the questions most frequently asked by girls is, "Should a girl kiss a boy on their first date?" It might be answered by asking them what they want a kiss to mean. Is it something they use to pay off a debt, or do they want it to be an expression of affection?

A boy values a kiss about in proportion as it is hard to get—as he thinks he is the only guy she would kiss.

If it is too easy he is apt to feel like the boy who said, "Oh, kissing a girl is just like getting pickles out of a bottle. After you get the first few the rest come easy."

But if he feels that the girl wouldn't kiss a boy unless she really liked him (and that's a good thing to tell the boys), then when she does kiss him it will mean something. (Kisses that are the expression of affection probably help people grow into love.)

Petting

But not all kisses are simply expressions of affection. If kisses are too long or too frequent they are apt to be sexually stimulating—particularly to the boy. This often causes trouble. What often starts out as necking progresses to petting.

Everyone who necks should realize that petting is *natural* for sexually mature human beings. It is preparation for mating and the happiness that can result.

But nature is not concerned with happiness—happiness is our idea. Nature is only concerned that the oak tree have acorns that in turn grow into oak trees. It is only concerned that we have children who, in turn, grow into adults and have children.

Another thing that has led to considerable confusion is failure to distinguish between sexual *stimulation* and sexual *satisfaction*. Sexual stimulation is anything that intensifies the reproductive drive. In the past we have been inclined to think that the orgasm (ejaculation) relieves the tension built up by the stimulation and gives an intense feeling of pleasure. This was supposed to be "satisfying" and to fulfill the needs of the drive.

Recently it has begun to become clear to some of us that unless sexual release is associated with a feeling of love, it may be only very *temporarily* tension-reducing. In the long run it may actually be sexually *stimulating*, with real satisfaction painfully absent.

Masturbation

Less than a century ago masturbation was blamed for all sorts of physical and mental ailments. With better knowledge of disease, mental illness, and feeble-mindedness, science has gradually come to see masturbation as a *result* rather than a cause.

Manipulation of the genitals for pleasure is almost universal among boys at some time during the adolescent period, and to some degree among girls. It usually follows the sexual stimulation that comes from physical contact through petting or intimate dancing, from hearing or reading something sexually exciting, or from seeing something stimulating (this applies particularly to boys).

As might be expected, masturbation occurs most frequently during that period when we are sexually mature and not yet emotionally mature. We have a sex drive but we have not yet learned to direct it nor to relate our sexual energy to mature love relationships. Part of growing up emotionally is learning not only to direct our tempers, our fists, and our tongues, but our sexual energy as well.

It is obvious that the less we expose ourselves to

sexually stimulating situations the easier this control will be. On the other hand, it would be difficult indeed to avoid a certain amount of sexual stimulation in a culture in which "sex" is the number one attention-getting device in advertising and commercialized entertainment and in which petting is so widely practiced.

Perhaps the most important thing about masturbation is the thought and feeling accompanying it. Thinking of sex, love and marriage together increases motivation toward marriage. On the other hand, thinking of having sex relations with some "pickup" or prostitute might motivate one toward that kind of sex behavior. This is not only the worst possible preparation for happy sex relationships in marriage, since it is selfish and exploitative in nature, but it also involves a very real danger of contracting a venereal disease.

Choosing Companions

You will find it easier to develop control over your sex drive if you choose the companionship of people who have wholesome attitudes toward sex and have a wide variety of other interests. Avoid association with a group who think and talk a great deal about sexual intercourse and treat it as though it were a test of one's manhood.

It is not always possible to avoid such groups. For example, a boy in the armed forces said: "You hear so much talk about sex in the barracks that it gets you all steamed up and makes you wonder sometimes whether it's worth waiting until marriage." When he was asked if he thought it would solve the problem if he did go out and have intercourse, this boy thought for a moment and then replied, "No, it wouldn't, would it? It would only make it worse.

"Actually," he went on, "there are fellows over there that are flunking right out of college, right out of their chances to be officers in the Navy because they can't get their mind off sex. The more they chase around the more they think about it. The more they think about it the more they chase around."

Girls too should be wary of boys who talk much about sex. It may be a "technique" looking toward conquest. It is probably wise to avoid a discussion of sex on a date. Such discussions are most profitable in groups, and best in groups where there is an adult present to restrain the individual who might introduce an off-color note, and to see that those who have reasons for restraint have a chance to state their case.

Those who lack restraint can seldom give reasons. They operate just on impulse, instinct, or selfish "desire."

The boy who talks a lot about sex frequently has developed it as an attention-getter. It is only a small step from that to manufacturing "conquests" to impress his listeners. More than one girl has found herself with a bad reputation because of her association with a boy who made up tall tales to impress others.

Certainly every girl should know that it is unlikely that a boy with whom she has intercourse will keep it a secret. Few boys can resist the impulse to tell someone of their conquest.

Girls Set Standards

Girls should recognize that in the last analysis they have to set the standards. Every girl has a deep-seated inhibition against promiscuity that no boy has, which comes from the fact that it is the woman who bears the child.

Many boys consciously, and many more unconsciously, tend to "try a girl out" when they go with her. The time to stop such activity is when it starts. Fortunately, a girl can usually tell when a boy is beginning to think of her sexually. If you want him to think of you in terms of friendship, and possibly later of love and marriage, you should act in a way that will demand his respect.

If you are very clear in your own mind that you have no intention of having sex relations, the vast majority of boys will respect you for it. But a boy dislikes the girl who goes out and pets and gets him aroused and then stops just short of intercourse.

The sexual tension built up in him is apt to cause him to become a "caveman"—or at least to quarrel with the girl and to dislike her. If he goes out with her again, it is probably because he knows that sooner or later she will "go too far."

Boys have for years assured girls that there was no danger of pregnancy the first time they had intercourse. Just the opposite is probably true if a girl is physically mature. A woman's sex desire is often

greatest at the time the ovum leaves the ovary and
starts through the tubes. If under this unusually strong
feeling she finally breaks down and "gives in," possibility of pregnancy is very great. Girls who allow
themselves to be thoroughly aroused run the risk of
pregnancy.

Furthermore, a girl should realize that if she doesn't
set standards it is she who will get hurt. Soon she
gets a reputation, and only boys who are seeking sexual
experience date her. You should be able to recognize
clearly the difference between popularity and noto-
riety.

Boys Have Standards, Too

Boys, too, must have ideals if they are to become
the kind of men who will be attractive to the kind of
girl they may some day want to marry. Girls still prefer
gentlemen, and there is much the average boy needs
to learn about how to be attractive to girls if he is
to be popular with them.

Too many boys cover up a lack of knowledge by
"acting smart"—which shows that they want to impress the girls but just don't know how. The boy who
is really smart watches the fellows that both guys
and gals *like*, and tries to understand why.

He usually finds such a boy interested in others
and willing to go out of his way to be helpful. Because
this boy is thoughtful of girls and treats them with
respect, they respect him. Because he tries to see that
girls have a good time on his dates, they are anxious
to date him again, so he seldom has to worry about
dates.

You may discover that girls will neck a little with a boy like that because they know he won't try to go any further, whereas they probably wouldn't even date a boy with the reputation of being a wolf.

Even more important, boys who are interested in girls as "friends" rather than as "females" will find that there are many things they can do together that are not only fun, but help them to discover many new types of activity they can enjoy. This helps in learning to know what type of girl to date, to go steady with later, and, still later, to marry.

The boy who "only wants to pet" is due for years of frustration—from almost every angle. The boy who really enjoys the companionship of girls in many forms of recreation such as sports, music, hobbies, etc., will find adolescence a lot of fun—and a period of real preparation for successful marriage.

Closer To Marriage

In a wholesome courtship where two people really enjoy each other, after about a year they grow into love. As they become more intimate, they naturally desire to express their affection more.

Unless they exercise a certain amount of control, this impulse tends to become increasingly stimulating sexually. When stimulation reaches a certain intensity it becomes unpleasant. Then there is a strong desire to relieve it by getting married or by having intercourse.

If two young people have started going steady at

too early an age and are not ready for marriage, either emotionally or economically, the mounting tension tends to result either in a quarrel or in sex relations. If they are old enough or sufficiently mature, this mounting tension may be the deciding factor in "making up their minds" to get married. If they started going steady too young this frequently means the desire to get married is stronger than the desire to finish their education, so they drop out of school.

This urge is natural and easy to understand. But it should be curbed, if only for economic reasons. Statistics show that the less education a man gets, the less he earns.

Dr. Henry Bowman studied the problem of divorce for ten years. He discovered that in over half of all divorces the couple had been in a hurry. Either they had started going steady too early, had become engaged before knowing each other long enough, hadn't been engaged long enough, or weren't old enough when they married. He concluded that most divorce is due not so much to marriage failure as *courtship* failure—that if the two people involved had really had a satisfactory courtship one of two things would have happened: They would have been better prepared for marriage. Or they would have discovered that they did not have the common interests, common ideals, common religion, common backgrounds that tend to assure marriage success.

The greater the difference in ideals, in intelligence, in education, in religion, in racial or cultural backgrounds, the more adjustments have to be made if the marriage is to succeed.

Sex During Engagement

Many young people who would not think of being promiscuous wonder about the wisdom of having sex relations before marriage with the person to whom they are engaged.

Dr. Noel Keys made a survey of all of the studies relating to marital happiness. "Nine out of ten of them," he declared, "indicated that our chances of a happy marriage appear better if we have not had sex relations before marriage. This is true for both the man and the woman."

Another study indicated that where a woman had sex relations only with the person she later married, it did not seem to interfere with marital happiness. We should remember, however, that the study ignored the many engaged couples who planned to marry but who developed conflicts over sex and never did.

There are several reasons why many authorities hold that sexual relations during the engagement period are unwise.

One of the factors urging the man into marriage is his sex drive. To the degree that he satisfies it outside of marriage his urge is lessened. Just the opposite apparently happens to the girl. Because of the insecurity regarding the permanency of the relationship, because of the ever-present danger of pregnancy, her drive toward marriage is intensified by illicit sexual relations.

But as soon as a girl begins to put on pressure, the boy is apt to react with, "What's the hurry?" She begins to wonder whether he really loves her and, apparently, he does, too.

Even engaged couples need to limit their physical expression of affection for each other when it approaches petting intensity. Tensions once aroused are hard to control.

For example, one girl found that after being out with her fiance, she for some reason began to cry. She sobbed and sobbed before she could get quieted down. She couldn't understand why, because she wasn't unhappy. The fact is that her crying was a method of releasing tension that resulted from too much petting.

The more a boy loves a girl in a mature and wholesome way the more he is likely to exercise control before marriage. But the more a girl loves a man the more she wants to please him. Men have often taken advantage of this by professing love they did not really feel. (See the last chapter for further discussion of this point.)

Learning To Choose

Day in and day out we must make choices. The person who attempts this without a set of principles is constantly overpowered by problems. But if we develop a set of principles, a set of moral standards, we are deciding in advance what we want to do with our life, how we want to live, and how we want to act in specific situations.

When a problem arises we simply stack it up against this set of standards or ideals and the decision is usually easier to make, thus saving us a lot of time and nervous energy. People who live without such a set of principles make hard work of practically every problem.

And yet we recognize that there are some situations that are not clearly black or white. It is on these particularly that we must use our heads. The thing we have to be careful of is that we do not choose the easy way simply because it is easy. Evidence is accumulating that happy and successful people use their intelligence to make choices in terms of long-range happiness rather than on the immature basis of "I want what I want when I want it."

Fortunately, most of us have been brought up with a set of principles that saves us from much unhappiness due to trial and error. We must learn from other people's mistakes because, as one person put it, "We don't live long enough to make them all ourselves." We can also learn from our own mistakes and successes.

Strong characters are built by learning to want to do what we ought to do, and not doing, even though we may want to, the things we know we ought not to do. Every time we do what we know we shouldn't, we lower our self-esteem and our confidence in ourselves.

Nothing you can do is worth what it costs if it injures your self-esteem. What you think about you is one of the most important things in determining happiness.

If you are a boy who treats all girls with respect,

they will respect you. If you see that they have a good time on a date, they will all welcome another date with you—and when you marry you will probably choose a girl who will be a wonderful wife and mother.

And then you will enjoy all the pleasures of real love. But what *is* "real love"? Let us talk more about it in the next chapter.

CHAPTER 4

So You Think It's Love?

By RALPH G. ECKERT

MANY YOUNG PEOPLE these days are confused by a pattern that has developed gradually during the last century or so. Psychologists have come to refer to it as "the romantic pattern" of love and marriage. We find it in most popular songs, novels, and motion pictures.

One old popular song, for example, went something like this: "If you look into her eyes and your heart sighs, that's really love." Wouldn't it be nice if it were really so easy to tell!

We have had the short story and the novel for many years, but in the last two generations we have developed new powerful influences—the motion pictures and TV. Most of us have been more influenced by them than we realize.

In a typical movie, for example, boy meets girl. They fall in love at first sight (they have to because there is only an hour and a half for the entire movie). Then a few problems are introduced to hold the audience in suspense. In the closing minutes, all these

From *"So You Think It's Love!"*, *Public Affairs Pamphlet No. 161* problems and obstacles must be overcome so that the picture can close with a grand clinch and the implication that "they lived happily ever after."

Is this a realistic picture of how happy marriages are formed?

Love At First Sight

Is there such a thing as "love at first sight"? When asked this question by a teenager, Dr. Oliver Butterfield, author of several books on marriage, replied, "I think it is a much better idea to take a second look." Actually, what usually passes for love in the romantic pattern couldn't possibly be love.

Take this typical movie: In the first few minutes of the picture the boy posed as somebody he really wasn't and obtained the girl's telephone number and address. He showed up at her home that night to try to get a date with her but found there was a party on. So he "crashed" the party.

The girl was furious with the boy both for crashing the party and for having deceived her that morning, so she set out to humiliate him. She put him in one embarrassing situation after another, but he was so conceited and ill-mannered that he wasn't embarrassed. Instead he embarrassed everybody else.

Just about the time you begin to wonder when she was going to call in her father or a cop and have him thrown out bodily, she swooned in his arms. Could that possibly be love?

Do We Fall In Love?

We have for a long time now used the phrase "fall-

ing in love"—as though you were going along and
something tripped you up. It is not anything you have
any control over, it seems, just something that happens to you.

Where did we get the idea that people can "fall
into love"? Apparently it goes back to the days when
people were apt to say, "Love is blind."

Actually, people do not *fall* into love, they *grow*
into love. What passes for love at first sight (and
what may eventually grow into love) is really *infatuation.*

Take the example of a girl who is just beginning to
date. She has not gone out with boys too often, but
she would like to believe that they think she is pretty
nice. Then a boy comes along who says some nice
things to her.

These compliments make her feel just wonderful.
She gets all excited and confused about this boy and
she thinks *he's* wonderful. She thinks she's in love
with him. (As a matter of fact, he has just made her
love herself a little more.)

If this girl is a well-adjusted person it will be natural
for her to respond to the boy's attention by treating
him wonderfully, too, since she thinks he's wonderful.
If they continue to be nice to each other, to make each
other feel respected and admired, and if they continue
going out together and find that they enjoy each other
in many different kinds of situations, they gradually
get to really know each other. They learn that they
definitely suit each other, and thus they gradually
grow into love.

Is It Really Love?

"How can we know it's really love?" This is one of the questions most frequently asked by young people, and most difficult to answer. Because love is not a specific thing—it is the total *feeling* we have about another person. To be sure that this feeling is really mature love we have to know, first of all, that it isn't just infatuation.

They used to call infatuation "puppy love." That was probably a pretty realistic term, because infatuation has about the same relationship to mature love that a puppy has to a mature dog—that is, it may become mature if it keeps on growing. But as one student put it, "It looks as though if you got married on 'puppy love' you'd be apt to lead a dog's life."

Remember, it takes time for love to grow, and the first test, therefore, is *the test of time.*

Secondly, to be sure it's really love we have to know that it isn't primarily physical attraction. It is natural to feel strongly attracted to somebody with whom we have been physically affectionate, such as in dancing, necking, or petting. A good test here is *the test of separation.* If you feel the same way about a person after you have been separated from him for weeks or months, that would be a favorable indication.

The third and final test is *the test of companionship.* What do you do when you're together? Do you find that you have a lot in common? If you enjoy doing all sorts of things together as *friends*, that is a good sign.

"Norma, how did you know?" one girl asked another who seemed to be happily married.

"Well," said Norma, "I knew we had lots of fun chasing around together, but I realized that I hadn't really ever seen him as a husband, only as an escort. We talked it over and decided that before we became engaged he should come over to my house every night for a week for dinner, then help me with the dishes and we would talk or read or listen to the radio afterward.

"We wanted to see whether we would get bored with each other. Or, if our attraction was primarily physical, whether we would be very frustrated by the lack of physical affection. By the end of the week we knew we would *enjoy* each other as husband and wife, and it has worked out that way."

A wise young couple—they used the test of companionship.

The test of "love" then is, how much do you really *enjoy* a person? How much do you care about his happiness? How much do you admire him? How much do you respect him? Is there normal physical attraction? Love *is* all of these, and more.

The "Right" Person

Another cause of confusion is the romantic belief that "when the right person comes along, you'll know it," as grandmother used to say.

Many young people think that love has to come suddenly and be romantic to be "really" love. Take for example the very attractive girl who had just received a letter from a boy overseas. In the letter he had asked her to marry him after he returned.

"Why, gee, we're more like brother and sister," the girl said. She described how they had grown up in the same block, practically next door to each other, had played "Kick the Can" and "Cops and Robbers," had gone through elementary school together, then high school, had belonged to the same church group, had even run around in the same crowd at times. "But we never dated each other," she exclaimed, almost with amazement. "It just wouldn't have occurred to us to date each other."

Then the boy had finished high school, had gone directly into the service, had his training, and had been sent overseas. All that time they had continued to write as brother and sister. After he had been over there about a year and had time to do some real thinking, he decided she was a pretty wonderful girl and the one he wanted to marry, so in one of their regular letters he popped the question.

"Gee," the girl concluded, "Mel's a wonderful fellow, but could you love anyone you know that well?"

She certainly could love someone she knew that well! In fact, we can't really *love* anyone until we do know him very well.

Dr. Paul Landis studied a group of hasty marriages (couples who had known each other only a couple of weeks) and found that four out of five of them ended in divorce within the first year. That doesn't look much like love at first sight, does it? Surely they *felt* they were in love or they wouldn't have married. What was wrong?

Becoming The Right Person

We know now that a happy marriage is not so much dependent upon finding the right person as on *becoming* the right person. People used to say that opposites attract each other. Now we know that the kind of person we are determines the kind of person we attract and are attracted to.

For example, here are three girls and here is one boy. The first girl just can't stand this particular boy. To her he is a "pain in the neck." The second one says, "Oh, he's all right—sort of a happy moron. But he's a lot of fun." But the third girl thinks he's wonderful. In fact, she has already decided she's going to marry him (although he doesn't know that yet).

Now, what is the difference? He's the same boy. Why does one think him intolerable, another wonderful? Isn't it because the boy meets one girl's needs but not the other's?

To the degree that you believe there is a "one and only" meant for you, you feel insecure. How in the world can you know which one it is, and how can you be sure that, like ships, you won't "pass in the night"?

But if you believe that a happy marriage results from being the kind of person who will attract the kind of person you want to marry, then you don't have to wait around for three, five, or ten years until the "right person" comes along. You can begin today to be the kind of person whom more and more people like to be around and whom eventually a great many people might like to have as a mate.

The idea that there is a "one and only" is nonsense.

Actually, the more people you like, the more people will like you and the more people there are with whom you could work out a happy marriage.

"Happily Ever After"

Still another source of confusion is summed up in the phrase "and they lived happily ever after." We began hearing that in the fairy stories we read as children. Unfortunately, too many adult stories or movies end with it.

Actually, the ill-mannered young man in the movie described earlier and the unpredictable young lady who "fell in love" with him could not possibly have lived happily together for more than a week or two. It is easy to dramatize the impulsive and the unpredictable to make a story entertaining, but in marriage these qualities are dynamite.

We enjoy being married to someone we can depend on, who is even-tempered, thoughtful, kind, considerate, helpful, friendly, honest, and affectionate. Unfortunately these qualities are difficult to dramatize. Young people have almost come to think of them as old-fashioned. Maybe they are, but people, too, are terribly old-fashioned. The same kind of people have been coming into the world with the same needs for thousands of years.

Probably nothing contributes more to our lifelong happiness than a happy marriage. But at the same time nothing can make us so completely miserable as an unhappy marriage. Too many young people brought up on the "romantic pattern" come to look forward to marriage as a state of perpetual bliss, or as a sort of "delicious insanity."

If you do, it can be guaranteed that you will be disappointed. There is no such thing as perpetual bliss. And no one wants to spend a lifetime in a state of insanity, delicious or otherwise.

CHAPTER 5

Too Young To Marry?

By LESTER A. KIRKENDALL

THE GRISWOLD HOUSEHOLD IS IN TURMOIL. Jim, the Griswolds' seventeen-year-old son, has just announced —quite obviously taking parental support for granted— his intention of marrying at Christmas time. He and Mary, his wife-to-be—Jim has assured his parents—are planning to continue their schooling, graduating together from high school the following June.

The Griswolds are far from being the only American family today weighing the arguments for and against an early marriage by one of its members. The number of such marriages has steadily increased.

In 1965, no less than 2.5 per cent of all men under 20, or 247,000 men, were married. In 1940 the percentage was only 1.4. The corresponding figures for women show that 10.3 per cent or 1,032,000 of the girls under 20 were married in 1965, while only 9.8 per cent were married in 1940. The rise was very sharp in the post-World War II years (13.7 per cent in

From "Too Young to Marry?", Public Affairs Pamphlet No. 236

1951). While the percentage of young women married has gone down since, with the natural increase in population it is clear that the *numbers* of teens getting married has climbed rapidly.

For years the median age of bride and groom at the time of their first marriage has been going down. The median age (the one at which half the people being counted are older, half younger) for women has dropped from 22.0 years in 1890 to 20.6 years in 1965. (This figure, too, was lower just after the war, indicating that brides were even younger then.) For men, the figure has gone from 26.1 to 22.8 years.

These figures contradict the belief that the heyday for early marriages was your great-grandfather's and great-grandmother's time. People think that in those days boys were on their own at an earlier age and got married sooner. Actually, there are more early marriages today than ever before.

All of this is cold comfort, however, to the Griswolds, to Mary, and to Jim—as well as to the young people and parents in thousands of other American families in which the difficult and important question of an early marriage is being wrestled with. What knowledge, what insight, what assistance can they find as they weigh the advantages and disadvantages, as they contemplate the possible results of an early marriage?

The Significance of Age

The importance of age as a factor in the success of a marriage is very hard to determine. Yet there must be some age at which it can be said that an individual is too young to be ready for marriage.

Obviously a child of twelve is not ready to marry. Laws have to be based upon this kind of judgment. Each state has a minimum age below which marriage is forbidden. While this age varies from state to state, it is most often eighteen for boys and sixteen for girls if they have the permission of their parents. Not until a man is twenty-one and a woman is eighteen are they free to marry without parental consent.

It is hard to say, therefore, just what an "early marriage" is. In this discussion, however, marriages in which the husband is under twenty-one and the wife under eighteen will be regarded as early marriages.

When we look at the statistics again, it appears that we may well be concerned about the outcome of early marriages. Six different investigators have found that the chances for happiness in marriage were less in early marriages than in later ones. One of these investigators, Judson Landis, found that the "divorce rate was six times higher in the marriages where both spouses were under twenty-one, than in the marriages in which both spouses were thirty-one or over at the time of marriage."

Each of these investigators recognizes that while age is clearly related to success or failure in marriage, age alone is not the cause of success or failure. There are probably several reasons why early marriages have a less favorable prospect of succeeding.

Some young people may marry early because they are in rebellion against their families or society, or because they are impetuous and self-willed, or lacking in

judgment. Others may lack maturity and have little
experience in handling the necessary responsibilities.

Of course, unless experience brings more stability to
these persons, they may fail just as readily in marriage
at a later age.

Why Early Marriages?

One important reason for the greater number of
early marriages today as compared with a generation
ago is continued prosperity. Never before have teenagers found it so easy to get jobs that enable them to
support themselves, buy cars, and enjoy a high degree
of economic independence. Beginning with World
War II, there has been a continuing demand for their
skills and abilities.

A second important reason is the existence of many
pressures in our society that push young people toward
marriage at an early age. These pressures may vary
from individual to individual, but there is no doubt
of their existence.

One such pressure is the necessity for every able-
bodied young man to serve in the armed forces. Some
couples meet the threat of separation and possible
loss of each other by deciding to marry. This may seem
to give the couple a security they would not otherwise
have.

It may seem to the girl to insure her a husband.
There is talk of the "man shortage," and to some girls,
marrying their boy friends before they enter the service
is an important insurance.

Another pressure is that of sexual curiosity or actual
sexual involvement. Whether this is a greater force

than it has ever been is a matter of speculation. Those who work with young people know, however, that a sizable number of teenagers marry to satisfy their sexual curiosity or because the girl has already become pregnant.

In some communities a wave of early marriages may occur, like an epidemic. The experience of seeing many of their friends marrying and of hearing many discussions about marriage undoubtedly causes some young people to marry who might otherwise have waited.

Another reason for early marriage may be found in the emphasis placed upon the satisfactions of marriage and family life in our American culture. One has only to see the movies, watch television, read current newspapers and magazines, and listen to conversations to realize the importance given to marriage and family life. Youth can hardly escape the conclusion that entering marriage is achieving a state that is worth attaining as early in life as possible.

Also among the reasons for entering marriage at an early age may be personal factors of which the individual may be unaware. For example, a disproportionate number of early marriages appear to be escapes, or manifestations of rebellion. The desire to get away from a poor home, from severe parental restrictions, or from school is too often the real reason for marrying early. Marriage may appear to be such an exciting and glamorous adventure that some young people marry without really understanding what they are doing.

(But there are some early marriages based upon ✳ strong, genuine friendships that are contracted by mature, responsible young men and women. Such marriages have the best chance of enduring and of developing into happy, successful family relationships.)

Many Other Factors

No flat statement can be made about the outcome of any particular marriage. Each must be considered on the basis of its own merits and demerits, including many circumstances other than age.

Some factors that seem unrelated to age may compensate for the disadvantages of youth. What looks like too early a marriage, when studied again may not seem to be a bad risk after all.

For example, Sue Ellis, age sixteen, was contemplating an "early marriage," to the distress of her parents and relatives. Sue, however, was marrying a young man of twenty-six who was already established in his business. Both were mature for their age, had had considerable dating experience, and had had a protracted courtship and engagement period together.

Even though Sue was young, her parents finally gave their consent, believing that the stability and maturity of her husband would more than make up for any difficulties arising from Sue's youth. And so it proved.

You're Not Alone

The partners themselves are the people most directly concerned about whether their marriage is a

good or a poor one. Their future and their happiness
are at stake. In fact, they are so clearly affected by the
outcome of the marriage that they sometimes deny
that anyone else is, or has a right to be, interested.

But others are vitally concerned also—particularly
the two families of the young couple.

Ethel Maas couldn't see why "I haven't the right to
live my own life." She was very much upset when her
parents objected to her plan to marry a young man in
the military service whom she had met only six months
before and to whom she had been attracted immediately. Ethel married despite her parents' objections.
Now, a year later, she finds herself deserted, pregnant,
and penniless. Her rosy dreams have disappeared, and
her parents are her only support, both emotionally and
financially.

There is no question now that Ethel's parents were
involved very deeply in her decision to marry.

In Ethel's case still another person is involved—her
child. In any marriage, successful or unsuccessful, the
lives of possible children must be considered. Their
future happiness is very much influenced by the wisdom with which their parents entered into marriage.
Young people might make sounder choices if they considered that they were selecting not only a mate but
also the other parent of their future children.

Finally, society itself—that is, all of us—are affected
by the success or failure of early marriages. The
strength of a community and ultimately a nation is
affected by the quality of family life. If many families
are unstable and full of conflict, community and na-

tional strength ebbs. The community may be saddled with the financial and emotional problems of families that cannot or will not care for themselves. For these reasons, the community as a whole needs to be concerned about early marriages and what they contribute to the strength of community living.

Tensions and Strains

As we already mentioned, people have said that our grandparents and great-grandparents went in for early marriages, too—and seem to have done pretty well with them. It's difficult, of course, to compare conditions that face teen marriages in the 1960s with those in the 1860s. The strains and tensions on today's young couples appear, however, to be considerably more severe than those of a century ago.

In the first place, social conditions are much more complex now than they were at that time. Today's young people are more likely to be cut off from the help of their parents. Not many young men are able to take over and operate their fathers' businesses. There are fewer farms, blacksmith shops, or small businesses to provide such opportunities.

Few families today are able to give their children, at the time of their marriage, a quarter section of land or some other income-producing property. Parents may, of course, give their children money, but this can be spent quickly and foolishly. It does not have the stabilizing, steadying influence of a parcel of land or part ownership in a store.

Young couples today are likely to live at a distance

from their parents and other relatives. (This may reduce in-law interference, but it also reduces the possibility of help and support in time of crisis. Young husbands and wives who have to build their marriage among strangers, amid alien conditions and customs, very frequently find the tensions and strains increased by these circumstances.)

If the husband's period of service in the armed forces comes soon after marriage, a couple may find themselves facing a prolonged separation just at the time when, for the sake of good marital adjustment, they should be together working out their problems. Or they may be faced with the strain of frequent uprootings and moves.

Not all persons, of course, react to these difficulties in the same way. (Some couples seem to thrive on such experiences. Meeting and conquering adversities seem to strengthen their relationship.)

In the 1860s a young man was much more likely to marry a girl whose family had always lived in the community and with whom he had been somewhat acquainted, perhaps even from boyhood. The families of the two might easily have been friendly for years. In the 1960s many couples are marrying with little or no acquaintance with each other's family or community backgrounds. The chance of marrying someone outside one's own religious faith, or with a markedly different background, is very definitely increased as one increases the range of one's acquaintanceship and moves about the country.

A young person today often has to learn the many-sided aspects of his or her partner's personality *after* marriage rather than before. This may make a good marriage adjustment more difficult, especially for teen-age couples who have had limited experience in working out new patterns of adjustment and behavior.

The manner in which modern-day society has tended to exclude adolescents from adult company and walled them off in a society of their own has greatly complicated the problems of mate selection for teenagers. In the adolescent society in which the teenagers live, people rate or fail to rate in accordance with standards that sometimes have little to do with success in adult and family life.

A boy may rate because of his athletic prowess, the smoothness of his line, or the sleek car he drives. A girl may rate because of her physical beauty, her skill in repartee, or her capacity for showing boys a good time. These are values that may prove relatively useless in family life later on. If these are the primary ones on which selecting a mate is based, there is a good chance the marriage will fail.

The greater the opportunity young people have for becoming familiar with adult society, the better will be their chance of developing a set of values that will stand them in good stead in choosing a marriage partner.

Pros and Cons

The desirability of early marriage has led to a great deal of controversy. The subject is debated hotly everywhere. You have probably heard each of the following statements made with great conviction by those arguing for or against early marriage.

People are more flexible and better able to adjust when they marry early. This is often used as an argument to support early marriage. But it has little force, since it is usually used to justify marriage now as against one which might occur two or three years later.

There would be little change in flexibility over such a short period of time, and older youth actually has more flexibility as well as greater experience.

The argument is of questionable validity even when youthful marriages are compared with the marriages of persons considerably older. Older persons have been discovered to possess much more flexibility than was formerly thought. Moreover, the process of becoming less flexible is a very gradual one, and not inevitable.

Flexibility is probably more the result of experience than of age. Some teenage people are quite rigid and inflexible. Some persons, because of their increasing range of experience and deepening insights, are more adaptable at twenty-six or sixty-six than at sixteen. We know that flexibility is largely a personal matter, varying with the individual.

Parents should have their children while they are young so that they can be better companions to them. This argument, also, while it has some point, should contrast an early marriage with a late marriage to have any real merit. Even then, the extent to which it is true will vary greatly with the individual. When it is used to support a marriage at sixteen as against one at twenty it becomes practically meaningless.

It would be more to the point to say that children need *mature* parents than to say that they need young parents. It is more important to be able to give the kind of companionship that will insure the child's best development.

Successful parents need to have completed their own adolescence. They need insights about child rearing that are based on more than good will. They need to know how to give their children emotional security and how to build in them the sense of trust and confidence essential to sound maturing. In general, persons who have passed their teens are readier for successful parenthood than those who have not.

The kind of person one might find acceptable as a mate during one's teens may be very different from the kind one will want later. This point, while having considerable merit, is usually based on a wrong assumption—that your personality changes so markedly in the span of a few years that your demands in personal relations cannot be predicted. There is no evidence to support the belief in such a change, nor do we expect it in other relationships. We do not think, for example, that young people who are getting along well with their parents when they are sixteen will have outgrown their interest in their parents in some mysterious way by the time they are twenty-five.

The problem is that many teenagers have either never thought through the characteristics they value in other persons, or have never had experiences that made them crystallize their thinking. They may still live wholly within their teenage world, unaware of which values and goals are important in adult life.

The characteristics of your personality are well established by the time you enter the teens. If a teenager has given careful thought to the values he holds and has some idea of the goals he will seek in life, he may be ready for marriage despite his youth.

A very young couple will be letting themselves in for some severe financial troubles. Whether this argument has any merit depends upon the circumstances of the couple contemplating marriage. Most inexperienced couples underestimate the costs of marriage. In that sense, at least, they are unready for the responsibilities of marriage. A realistic appraisal of the financial costs of the early years of marriage—including possible pregnancy and possible illnesses—would seem a part of marriage preparation.

There are other hardships besides financial ones that may be experienced in a marriage. Heavy labor, loneliness, and the renunciation of former interests may be accounted hardships. Whether they really are will depend on whether the couple regards them as such or not.

Nor should we seek to divest marriage of all its hardships. They can be unifying experiences if the couple meets them shoulder to shoulder. Rather than avoiding problems, what should be sought is strength and resourcefulness in meeting them.

The occupation and income of the couple may be fixed at a permanently low level. This is a very important consideration. Although the husband may seem to be the one chiefly affected, the living standard of the whole family is at stake. A youth who marries,

previously

having just graduated from high school with no trade or occupation, is likely to have to take a low-paying, unskilled job to support his family. Unless he has some outside help, he will be so busy keeping ahead of the bill collector that he may never be able to continue his education.

Some youthful couples attempt to cope with this problem in one of two ways. Some of them try to postpone the coming of children while both work to build up the family resources. Others plan to marry but continue their education. Both of these methods will be discussed at length later.

Early marriage is a safeguard against sexual experimentation and promiscuity. This argument assumes that any marriage, even a bad one, is better than sexual experimentation. It also assumes that marriage will prevent both experimentation and promiscuity, which is not necessarily true. A happily married couple will not be likely to engage in extra-marital sexual activities, but this is hardly a conclusive argument for an early marriage.

"We are in love." This argument is the most potent of all in the opinion of many people both young and old, yet it is probably more in need of careful examination than any of the other arguments.

Hundreds, even thousands of young people have been disillusioned by having what they thought was "love" turn into coldness and indifference or even into bitterness and hatred. The figures on the break-up and failure of early marriages indicate that a larger proportion of teenage youth have this experience than do older persons. The problem of deciding if it is really love is particularly acute for young people considering teenage marriage.

Love's Confusions

This burning question has been discussed in previous chapters, but the possible confusions of "love" are especially important to teenage marriage. Let's go into them a little more deeply:

— *Love may be confused with having fun.* A couple in love should certainly be able to have fun together. Simply being able to have such fun, however, does not prove that two people are in love or will make suitable partners for each other in marriage. Yet we are often confronted with couples who, having had a rollicking good time on a number of dates, feel that they are "made for each other."

The qualities that make two persons good partners in play or in recreation are not necessarily the same qualities that will enable them to carry financial responsibilities together or to be a good team in the rearing of children.

Two persons may be divine dancing partners, yet one may be a spendthrift and the other a skinflint. They may play on the beach with complete enjoyment, yet one may be very lax in the handling of children and the other exceedingly strict. The way they handle their finances and work with their children is likely to have much more effect on their marriage than the way they dance or trade jokes.

The activities of a couple after marriage are usually

quite different from those before marriage. Consequently, judgments made on the basis of liking the same activities before marriage may be very questionable. A married couple is usually so occupied with making a living, with working out marital adjustments, and with rearing children that they lack time, desire, and money for the fun-making and recreational activities in which they engaged before marriage.

Love may be confused with glamour. Our society makes so much of dating, getting engaged, and the wedding that the excitement of getting into the pre-marriage whirl sweeps some young people off their feet. They feel somewhat like the girl who said "I don't know whether I'd like to be married or not, but I would like to have a wedding."

There is also the glamour that may come with having captured a partner who is particularly choice in the eyes of one's friends. More than one boy has been married because he was a football hero rather than for his qualities as an individual. More than one girl has been married for her success in a popularity contest rather than for qualities of personality and character.

One girl pointed up this confusion between love and glamour when she analyzed her broken marriage.

"I had known Don throughout our four years of high school, but never dated him until the latter part of our senior year. That year I was elected Queen of the May and was crowned in a gorgeous coronation ceremony.

"As I stepped down from the stage after being

crowned, Don met me at the foot of the stairs. He asked me for a date and I agreed to go out with him the next week. On the date he said that when he saw me being crowned queen he knew he loved me."

True movie style! From this first date the two quickly married, only to have it break up a year later because:

"He made fun of me and my parents. He thought my standards foolish and called me highbrow. He really wanted nothing in life beyond a car and a good time. When he hurt me, he never apologized but took even more advantage. I couldn't respect him."

Love may be confused with sexual attraction. This is possible especially when the physical aspects of the relationship, petting or intercourse, become a part of the picture early or are heavily relied upon for satisfaction in the relationship. Through petting or actual sexual relations, a boy and girl may arouse such strong sexual desires that they are no longer able to make sound judgments about themselves as a couple. They are unable to tell whether they are entranced with sex or with the whole individual.

One finds couples involved in intercourse who are unable to talk frankly and honestly about sex and their sexual relationship. They do not know for certain how the other feels about the relationship. They are conscious of taking advantage of the other person in some way, yet are unable or unwilling to curb their desires.

In many instances couples go ahead sexually, assuming that in the event of pregnancy they will marry. The girl may accept intercourse with the expectation that it will lead to marriage. In these situations the emphasis on sex may prevent the couple from making an intelligent choice of marriage partners.

Love may be confused with sharing miseries. Many of us have seen situations in which two young people from miserably unhappy homes come together, begin to speak of their unhappiness, and in not too long a time are married.

Such marriages may be the result of confusing love with sharing miseries. Marriage partners should be able to share unhappinesses, but such sharing is not in itself love.

Love may be confused with a desire for escape or rebellion. Young people in their teens often face a lot of obstacles to growing up and becoming independent. Laws require them to attend school until a certain age. Parents set certain limits on their actions. It seems hard sometimes to gain the recognition they feel they ought to have as young adults.

Some young people find themselves in situations in which they are very unhappy. They may have to do more work than they feel is fair. Their school work may seem pointless. They may feel that they will never become really free, or never be able to earn their own money and spend it as they wish.

Parents may seek to keep a child dependent upon them. If he talks about marriage, the parents are likely to forbid it or at least to disapprove strongly. Under such circumstances a young person is likely to regard marriage as an escape and express his rebellion by pushing as rapidly as possible toward marriage.

Love may be confused with jealousy and possessiveness. Many people feel that jealousy and a desire to possess are evidence of love. Actually they are more an evidence of insecurity or of a desire to control and dominate. They are never sound emotions upon which to build a marriage. The kind of love that an enduring marriage can be based upon should seek to free the other person and at the same time to protect him in this freedom.

Teenage people, girls particularly, often behave in such a way as to provoke jealousy, and only then are convinced that love is genuine. They are pleased at manifestations of jealousy, thinking that this means true love. What they cannot sense is the way in which continued jealousy can become a kind of imprisonment. The jealous person uses his feelings to cut his partner off from others.

Love may be confused with a desire to defeat someone else. Many times teenage dating is strongly competitive. Bill, for example, married Ellen after an arduous courtship in which he was competing with four other fellows for her attention. Being of a competitive nature, he found the rivalry very exciting. "She was a real prize." Yet within six months after their marriage Ellen realized why Bill had married her, and Bill himself had lost practically all interest in the marriage.

Love may be confused with a desire to hurt someone else. Some youthful marriages occur "on the rebound." Someone who has been dropped by his dating partner may marry another person within a matter of weeks. It is often a way of salving hurt pride, and of saying to the offender, "I don't care for you, and you don't matter, as you can plainly see, since I'm marrying someone else."

A period of calming down after a break-up is a good thing. A person who commits himself too deeply to a new relationship while still upset over a break with someone else runs a chance of making a serious mistake.

Love may be confused with material gifts. Gifts may be a genuine expression of love. They may also be a way of trying to obligate the receiver or to insure the outcome of a relationship. In addition to gifts, one needs to look for evidence of genuine respect, friendship, and love.

"Go Slow" Signs

In contemplating an early marriage there are some "go slow" signs that are worth noting before the final decision is made.

"Go slow" when there is a feeling that it is "get married now or never." Young people planning marriage are often very impatient with any suggestions that seem to involve a delay in marriage. Yet the urgency that some of them feel is often a reflection of uneasiness and insecurity. They half realize that something is amiss, yet they dare not stop and examine their difficulty.

A postponement now need not mean the marriage is off for good. But if that should be the result, it probably was a marriage that should not have taken place.

"Go slow" when there is a one-sided feeling. Sometimes one of the partners-to-be is eager for marriage while the other is lukewarm or reluctant. When one partner has to urge or persuade the other, something is usually wrong. A marriage in which one of the mates is a reluctant partner is almost certainly in for trouble.

"Go slow" when your intention is to reform your partner. Sometimes one or both of the partners marry with a secret intent to change or make over the other. This is likely to lead to trouble. You should be able to accept your partner as he is before marriage. If you cannot, then it is best to call off the marriage or wait until you can accept him. There will be some minor changing and adjusting after marriage, but it would be wholly unrealistic to expect a major overhaul job.

"Go slow" when there are strong parental objections. There should be a careful analysis of the underlying reasons for the parents' objections. The parents may fear the sacrifices they think their child will have to make. They may dislike the thought of giving up their child. They may see some serious handicap to the marriage. In any case, both parents and young people should try to get at the basic causes for the objection.

Teenagers sometimes find themselves pushed toward marriage by close friends who insist that it is a good match and that parental objections should be ignored. This advice, too, should be examined carefully. Many times it merely reflects the problems of the persons giving the advice. They are eager themselves to marry or to gain freedom from their parents. Not being in a position to gain these ends themselves, they get satisfaction from seeing someone else accomplish them. But their advice is not objective or unbiased.

"Go slow" even when there is a pregnancy. When this occurs with a couple planning to marry anyway, the usual solution is to marry immediately. Unfortunately, pregnancy sometimes occurs with couples who have not been planning to marry or who are not sure they wish to marry. A common solution is to advise a couple in this situation to go ahead and marry.

This may be only a way of sentencing this couple and their child to a lifetime of unhappiness in a mismated marriage. In some instances the marriage soon breaks.

Other couples may resort to illegal abortion, but this is a dangerous way to meet the situation. It puts the girl at the mercy of unscrupulous doctors or quacks. Others may plan to let the girl have her baby and then place it for adoption. Sometimes the child is kept by the mother with the help of relatives.

There is no invariable answer as to what is best to do in the event of a premarital pregnancy. Too often the young people feel it is impossible to talk with their families, and they try to handle the situation themselves. See a doctor first. Then it would be wise to talk with someone with counseling experience: a social worker, a psychologist, a psychiatrist, or a minister.

Some Drift Into Marriage

Some young people marry because they do not know how else to work out their relationship. Sometimes couples drift along from month to month, all the time becoming more committed to each other and finally to marriage. One or both may feel a sense of dissatisfaction with the relationship, yet be unable to discuss it for fear of hurting the other's feelings.

The longer an undesirable relationship goes on, the greater the hurt when it finally does break. No one can live through a lifetime continually covering up his real feelings. It is always better to talk honestly and frankly even at the expense of possible hurt feelings or even a broken relationship.

The problem is often complicated by the eagerness of a couple to announce their engagement publicly. The gay whirl of events—announcements, parties, showers, happy congratulations—seems so attractive that they cannot wait to make their announcement until they have thoroughly analyzed their own plans. Having made a public announcement, the couple is likely to find the pace of events leading to marriage so rapid that they cannot do any real planning. They are also likely to find that it becomes very difficult to withdraw from their plan to marry if they should decide they want to. A couple is wise to let public announcements, engagement rings, and acceptance of gifts await a careful and thorough study of their decision to marry.

An unwillingness to move slowly and carefully along the path to marriage is in itself a "go slow" sign.

Financial Help From Parents?

Suppose a couple has decided upon an early marriage. What are the problems that then arise?

The first may very well be the need for financial

help from parents. Such assistance these days is sometimes referred to as a "subsidy," with the implication
that it is something quite different from what used to
be done. Actually, it is a very old practice.

In some cultures a dowry in the form of goods or
money went with the bride. Earlier in our own history
it was common in rural districts for a family to give
a parcel of land to their children when they married.
This provided them with a place to live and a source
of income. An urban family might take a son into
partnership in a business when he married.

Today most urban families derive their support
from salaried jobs. Parental assistance to a young
couple more and more has to take the form of direct
financial help, or practical gifts to the young people
for setting up housekeeping.

Many families do help their young people in this
manner. While this is a decision for each individual
family to make, there seems no reason why such a
plan should not be considered by families with young
people about to marry.

There should be a clear and mutually acceptable
understanding between the parents and the young
couple concerning the conditions under which the
assistance is given. Is it to be repaid? Is interest to
be charged? How long will the help continue? Is it a
gift?

The fear is sometimes expressed that financial aid
will make the young couple dependent, that it will
undermine their self-reliance. This argument deserves
some analysis.

No one would argue that a bank loan or an unexpected windfall of money from some outside source would do this. If assistance from the parents appears to have this result, then we must conclude that the young people were already overly dependent and the financial help changed that situation very little.

Parents can, however, extend assistance in such a way as to encourage independence. They might give a young married couple money, but at the same time help the couple work out a plan for financial independence as soon as practicable.

Actually, most young people are anxious to be independent of their parents. In some instances young couples refuse help from their parents because "there are too many strings attached."

In practice, parental aid to young couples may take many forms. The parents may help the couple get their furniture. They may make specified monthly payments for a period of time. If the parents own a farm, a grocery, or some similar establishment, they may give the couple some food or sell it to them at cost for a period of time. They may extend them a loan with specific provisions for its repayment. An amount of money may be given with the stipulation that it is an advance on the inheritance the child might have expected. The parents may continue the educational expenses for their child, particularly the amount that they had been planning to spend anyway.

Does Education Go On?

Shall the couple attempt to combine marriage and education? For some couples this will mean finishing high school. For others it will mean weighing the possibilities of going on to college. Obviously, the decision has to depend upon the goals of the young people and their capacities.

Certainly for those who can do it at all creditably, it would seem wise to finish high school. The number of jobs that do not require a high school education is getting smaller and smaller. A person without such an education may have a hard time.

Most high school marriages occur at a time when the young people have about a year of schooling left. It would seem wise to arrange to continue until graduation.

In some communities, opposition has been expressed to permitting married pupils to continue in high school. This opposition, however, is disappearing rapidly. Any attempt to deny education to married young people would probably be held illegal if a court test were made. Still, it would be wise for a youth of high school age to check upon the school's policy before marrying.

The question of continuing a college education presents no problem so far as acceptance is concerned. Every college campus has some young married couples who are continuing their education. The problem really becomes one of whether a particular couple can swing it financially. Before marrying, they should discuss the problem carefully, considering just what the burden will be on each of them.

A common arrangement is for the husband to continue his education while the wife finds some kind of work to support the family. In many instances the husband also finds work. In some cases both husband and wife arrange to continue in college while both work. This may mean that the couple will take longer than usual to complete their college education.

Under the best of circumstances, married couples who continue their education have to scrimp and pinch pennies, unless both work. The extent to which a couple is willing to accept lower living standards will be a factor to consider. Are they willing to do without a car, or a telephone? Can they forego trips home at vacationtime? Have they the stamina to stand up under continuous hard work with very little recreation?

Young married couples going to college find other young couples in the same boat. This usually helps to ease the problem. At least it isn't so hard to keep up with the Joneses.

No young couple ought to run from responsibility. Of course, responsibilities can become so heavy that they break the couple's spirit. But seldom does a marriage mean anything to the partners unless they have invested some effort, emotion, and even sacrifice in it.

It is a real question, however, whether the wife should be asked to give up her plans for an education. A decision to do this may work a real hardship on her and the family at some later period, especially if there comes a time when she has to support herself. A wife who works may also find that she is left behind, intellectually, while her husband moves ahead. The wife's working could thus become a dividing rather than a unifying experience unless the couple is aware of the problem and plan accordingly.

Sometimes couples who are planning to marry and continue their education base their plans on the assumption that a pregnancy will be avoided. This is unrealistic. It is also unfair to a child if one should come. A couple had better not marry if they feel that they just cannot afford to have children under any circumstances.

It may be wise for a couple to postpone their marriage for a year or two if they wish to complete their college education. They would be more mature when they did marry, and they would have had a chance to sample college social living as unmarried persons. There would be a shorter time to put up with a cramped standard of living, and less chance of a pregnancy interrupting their education. If they marry at the beginning of the junior year instead of the freshman year, they have a much better chance of completing the four years successfully.

Without doubt, the practice of combining marriage and education will become increasingly common. In all probability parents will become more and more willing to help pay the educational expenses of a son or daughter who marries before he or she is through school.

There is really no special reason why a person must complete his or her education before marrying. While this has been the convention, experience indicates that marriage may result in a frame of mind that makes a person an even better student.

Combining marriage and education is practical from some points of view. The problem is one of realistic and careful planning.

Having Children

Many young couples have a child within the first year of marriage. A young couple facing problems of adjustment and having to take up heavier responsibilities than they are used to carrying need time to work things out. In many instances they would be much better off if they can delay the beginning of a pregnancy until they have had a chance to make a satisfactory adjustment to each other and to married life.

If their religion does not permit a couple to use contraceptives, the effect of an early pregnancy on their plans needs to be studied very carefully. Even when contraceptives are used, they are sometimes ineffective, sometimes incorrectly used. And sometimes the young people have been too inhibited or too embarrassed to go to a planned parenthood center or to discuss the subject with a doctor—or even to talk freely with each other about their sexual relationship.

When two people marry, they should have reached a point of objectivity about sex that enables them to ask questions and to talk about sex matters with competent persons, with a marriage counselor, a pastor, a doctor. Practically all physicians are able to give technical information on contraception, but not all are able to help on the vitally important psychological and emotional aspects of sex adjustment.

In deciding how soon to have a child, one factor to take into account is the readiness of the young people to handle the responsibilities of parenthood. The nature and significance of these responsibilities are not likely to be understood unless the couple has had some actual first-hand experience with children. Talks with good parents and the reading of some good literature should be helpful.

The state of their finances and their educational plans are also factors young people have to consider when planning a family.

Ready To Settle Down?

Young people about to marry should ask themselves, "Are we really ready to give up our freedom and our present social life for marriage?" Young people may forget that the demands of marriage will require them to forego some of the things they prize.

They may want to marry because all of their friends are doing it or to satisfy their sexual desires, but they may be unready to settle down to everyday married life. One can see how a young wife who married before she had really had her fill of dating and nice clothes might make unfair demands on her marriage— or how a young husband, unready for marriage, might still insist upon spending most of his money on a car or on his hunting equipment.

Factors that make for success or failure in marriage are not all subject to control. A person may think he knows how well he can accept the need to scrimp in his marriage, yet he cannot be sure until the circumstances have arisen. This is not an argument for or against early marriage. It is simply a fact of which everyone should be aware. You will then be more ready and better able to meet the unexpected turn of events in your marriage.

CHAPTER 6

If You Marry Outside Your Religion

By ALGERNON D. BLACK

NOTHING IS MORE DEEPLY imbedded in American tradition than the right of a person to choose his mate freely without outside interference. Yet young people often find that the exercise of this right raises difficult problems, particularly if they happen to fall in love with persons with different religious backgrounds from their own.

To make matters worse, they often get conflicting advice. Some friends say: "Don't marry out of your church or religious group or you'll regret it the rest of your life. Religion goes deep. You can't compromise it."

But others insist: "Religious differences don't matter. Man and woman differ in many ways. It makes marriage interesting. You have to adjust. It isn't always easy. But love finds a way."

Should young people of different religions marry? How difficult is it to achieve contentment, happiness,

From "If I Marry Outside My Religion," Public Affairs Pamphlet No. 204

and mutual satisfaction when partners enter marriage with different childhood religious experiences and beliefs? The problem has become a real one for increasing numbers of young men and women.

Every marriage brings together persons from different families, ranks, classes, and other diverse traditional and cultural backgrounds. "Intermarriage" becomes a problem only when some element of difference is seriously disturbing to the marriage partners or to the groups to which they belong.

Before we consider the problem let us take a look at the marriage of one couple of different religious backgrounds.

Sally, a devout Roman Catholic girl, meets Jim, a less devout Lutheran young man. They have about the same levels of intelligence and education. Their home backgrounds are similar in many respects but different in others. But the main difference is in their religion.

Jim does not want to become a Roman Catholic. Sally does not want him to be coerced into changing his faith. The priest states the conditions under which a Catholic may marry a non-Catholic. Because of the haste and tension and manner of the declaration of "the conditions and requirements," the two young people are upset and arrange a marriage ceremony by a Justice of the Peace.

Within a short time the young wife becomes distressed over the fact that "this was not a real marriage." She attends her church, goes through Confession and Penance and Communion, and upon the husband's promise that the children will be brought up as Roman Catholics, the priest marries them.

But the matter does not rest there. Although their marriage has many of the elements of success, the differences over religion continue to crop up and to be a source of irritation. Jim's mother cannot reconcile herself to having her grandchildren raised as Catholics. Jim himself, though living up to his agreement, finds the arrangements increasingly distasteful.

At first Jim tries to bottle up his irritation, but this leads to unpredictable emotional upsets. He finds himself quarreling with Sally over unimportant and irrelevant matters when what he is really upset about is her insistence that the children be sent to a Catholic school—or perhaps it is the fact that the only friends who come to the house any more are Catholics. Later, under the goading of Jim's mother, the religious issue is brought out in the open as a frequent source of contention, until finally the marriage itself is torn by conflict.

This marriage undoubtedly could have been a happy one, as have thousands of others between partners of different faiths, if the partners had: (1) understood what they had to reckon with; (2) staked out their common ground; and (3) worked to make the marriage a success.

This particular situation has been mentioned not to dissuade anyone from a marriage outside his or her religion, but rather to illustrate some of the obstacles that must be overcome in such a union.

It was not the differing beliefs that caused the

trouble between Sally and Jim. They rarely do. When a couple is in love, when what they hold in common is stronger than the divergence in belief, such differences usually can be overcome. But when, as in the above case, there is pressure from one or both of the families, the situation gets harder to deal with. If a minister or priest intervenes, it may be tangled still further. Friends or the social group also may cause trouble where husband and wife come from circles that vary sharply in views, habits, and attitudes.

These are not insoluble problems, but you should consider them very carefully before marrying someone of a different denomination or religious faith. For unless you want to cut yourself off completely from your family, church, and friends, you will have to reckon with their influence as part of your future.

Interfaith Marriages Increasing

Despite pressures from home, church, social groups, and society in general, more and more young people are taking mates of other religious affiliations. It is estimated that today one out of every five marriages unites young people of different religious beliefs and ancestries.

There are a number of reasons for the increase in recent years. Among them are:

1. The increasing freedom of the individual to move about and to choose his own friends.

2. The concentration of populations in larger towns and urban communities so that the individual and the family meet many different kinds of persons,

whereas in smaller and more isolated communities they met only their own kind.

3. The increased mobility of the individual through improved transportation and the increased number of contacts in neighborhood living, in industry, commerce and the professions, and in recreational and civic community activities.

4. The lessened use of the home as the center for recreational life and social contacts, and of the family circle as the setting in which the young establish their social contacts with the opposite sex.

5. The fact that within a given community there may be a scarcity of eligible and compatible young people of the same religious group. For a woman particularly, the only way to marry a man of improved social or economic status may be to go outside the traditional religious group.

6. The increased number of women working and earning, making it possible for them to meet more men of diverse backgrounds and to be less passive in the process of choosing a mate.

7. The lessening of discrimination and segregation in housing, education, and employment, making it possible for young people to meet and know one another in work and study and play and to break through the old patterns of separation and prejudice.

Changing Attitudes

These changing attitudes—partly the result of changed conditions—also have contributed:

1. Educational programs and social experiences in

some areas have stressed respect for differences, and for equality of rights regardless of color, creed or national origin.

2. Religious programs have stressed interfaith cooperation and the brotherhood of man.

3. The democratic ideal of a community, enriched by the unity and cooperative relations of human beings of diverse gifts and backgrounds, appeals to young people as the only sound basis for happiness and peace.

4. The bond between young people and the religion of their birth often has been weakened by the failure of the religious organization to meet the needs of the young.

5. Although the orthodox and authoritarian leaders of all sects oppose and try to prevent intermarriage by preaching and indoctrination and penalties, they all permit it under certain conditions. Some of the more liberal religious sects appear to have few restrictions and are quite prepared to see their young people marry members of other faiths. Their ministers are quite ready to perform the ceremony, and the churches recognize it if it is performed by civil officers or by clergy of other faiths.

For a number of reasons, then, many more young people today than ever before face the question of whether to marry or not to marry someone of a different religious faith. As free human beings, the choice is theirs to make. But as with any other choice, it is wise to consider all the facts before making a final decision.

Hazards of Religious Differences

There are no national statistics to show just how the chances of an interfaith marriage compare with those of a marriage between persons from the same religious fellowship. Even if there were, you probably would not find the information very helpful as a guide to your own prospects. For every couple is different from every other.

We all know that the general divorce rate today is high. But few of us would let the statistics on divorce frighten us out of marriage altogether.

Experience, however, does provide helpful guideposts. Such studies as have been made indicate that the more similar the background, interest, and beliefs, the more likely the success of the marriage. One study, covering a fairly small sample, indicates that the rate of failure is somewhat higher in mixed marriages than in marriages between members of the same faith.

At first glance these figures seem fairly conclusive. But when examined closely, they are difficult to interpret. Is the failure of these marriages due to strong religious convictions and conflicts over religious issues? Or is it due to other factors—the adjustment of man and woman living together, different physical and emotional needs, personal habits, early training, differences of taste and values, attitudes toward decisions involving vocation, leisure time, friends, finances, relations to in-laws?

Or is the failure due to external factors, the pressures of families and religious groups and the community as a whole? Is it possible that the opposition to intermarriage is so strong in many American communities that it affects employment or social contacts or educational opportunities of the two people involved till it strains the marriage bond to the breaking point?

Religious Conflict May Hide Real Problems

Feelings over religious differences may become intense enough to wreck a home. But usually no one factor can make or unmake a marriage. The strength of this bond depends upon a number of elements.

Often the husband and wife give reasons for their marriage difficulties that are far from the heart of their trouble. Frequently, an issue over which there is much conflict and unhappiness is merely the combat area in which hostility is expressed. The true causes usually lie far below the surface. Thus religious differences may sometimes be thought to be the reason but much deeper currents of feeling are the real cause.

This may be seen in the following case:

A lawyer marries his secretary. He is of Jewish and she of Protestant background. Neither is religious in any traditional sense. Both families are unhappy about the marriage. The Christian family rejects the Jewish son-in-law and their daughter. The Jewish family resists the marriage, but they finally accept it. They attend the wedding, help the couple set up their home, and are glad to welcome their new daughter and the grandchildren as their own.

As the years pass and the children grow up, the

pressures for membership in a Christian church and in the Jewish temple increase. It is a suburban community and the religious and social lines are sharp. Even though the Jewish lawyer has an overwhelming majority of non-Jewish clients, the great body of these have no social relationship with him or his wife. Their chief contact with their neighbors is in the Parent-Teacher Association at the school, in the Community Chest, and in the shops.

The wife resents the rejection of her children, who are attractive, gifted, and popular in school, but labeled "Jews." Neither husband nor wife is informed concerning his or her own ancestral faith. Neither knows much about the faith of the other. The religious issue is never an occasion for conflict. Both partners agree that the children should be brought up with knowledge of the Jewish and Christian beliefs and should respect all faiths as equal.

But there are troubles in this marriage. Many acquaintances say that the troubles are due to the difference of religion, but the difficulty lies deeper. The husband comes from a family of great wealth, a family of professional people with a tradition of learning, liberalism, sophistication. The wife in this instance comes of a family of moderate means and from a fairly conservative, small-town community. She has not had much opportunity for higher education.

Though she has been a good home manager, companion, and nurse, the wife feels inadequate intellectually. The husband has turned more and more to his practice and to his business and professional interests. As the children have reached adolescence and the independence of high school and college, the wife has felt more and more lost. Conflict has arisen.

Some will point to this family as a good example of successful mixture—while others will find here an example of the failure of religious intermarriage. In reality, the deeper questions are: Why did this man, with his unusual combination of qualities, feel the need and desire to marry this girl of a background different from his, not only religiously, but socially, financially, and culturally? Why has the community persisted in labeling and rejecting a woman of Christian ancestry as a "Jew"?

What Are the Chief Obstacles?

The chief obstacle to a successful religious intermarriage is psychological. Marriage is an adjustment. Even the most perfect marriage has its moments of difference and misunderstanding.

Religious issues also may be the occasion of conflict within a marriage of people of the same faith. Even where Roman Catholics accept the same basic doctrines, they may quarrel over the degree of religious observance, church attendance, financial contributions, parochial or public school education, and the interpretation of church policy and attitudes toward members of other faiths. So, too, Protestants of the same denomination may cross swords over religious issues and a Jewish husband and wife may find that their common acceptance of Judaism does not necessarily mean complete agreement on religious matters.

When a man and woman are drawn to one another, select one another from among many, feel a physical attraction and a congeniality and an affection amounting to a deep hunger, there are many factors that determine whether this relation will be healthy, happy, and permanent. Common interests, some similarity in levels of intelligence, a sharing of basic values—these are more important in the long run than any particular difference on any particular day. When both partners are basically well adjusted people and love one another and share a common concern for the same values, there is a strong likelihood that they will be able to work out their problems.

Yet when this is said, it cannot be denied that a marriage concerns more than the husband and wife. The marriage involves the lives and relationships with the families and the religious communities in which the husband and wife had their origin and childhood associations. Although families, churches and communities have only an indirect influence, they can do much either to complicate and injure or to support and further the happiness of those concerned. Thus young people who contemplate a religious intermarriage should be fully aware of the pressure that may be brought on them.

What About the Families?

The parents of young people usually desire their children to hold their own basic outlook and faith and to marry those of like viewpoint and raise families within the fold. When questioned concerning the marriage of their sons, one study found that twenty out of one hundred of the fathers approved and eighty out of one hundred of the fathers disapproved selection of a mate from another faith. The mothers revealed the same attitudes, nineteen per cent approving and eighty-one per cent disapproving. In the marriage of daughters, fourteen per cent of the fathers approved and eighty-six per cent disapproved; of the mothers, fifteen per cent approved and eighty-five per cent disapproved.

In fact, many parents find it difficult to accept and approve *whatever* partners their young sons and daughters choose. This is natural and human. But it may be a cause for grave unhappiness, as in the following case:

The daughter in a Jewish family returns from college at the end of her freshman year and announces that she has "found her man." The young man is of Lutheran tradition.

The girl's father argues that he has no prejudice against Lutherans. He objects to so important a decision while she is only eighteen years old and while she is still far from finishing her college course. He argues that she has had far too little experience for a wise choice. The father pleads with the daughter to wait, take her time, think it over.

The young people elope and marry.

The girl's father is distraught. He insists that he has no objection to marriage with a member of another religion or tradition. He feels bitter that his daughter made a crucial life decision on the basis of the irrational and emotional needs of the moment.

Deeper than the reasons given by this father is the fact that the young man in question has had little ambition for an education and lacks the kind of energetic and dynamic drive that might assure a successful business or professional career. The father has always pictured his daughter's marriage as a union with someone of his own intellectual and vocational and financial achievements.

To many people this is an example of the failure of marriage between Jews and Christians. To those who observe more discriminately, it is evident that the issue is not religious but concerns, first, the preferences of parents in such matters as type of personality, intellectual and cultural levels, educational and vocational and financial considerations, and second, the haste, if not defiance, with which the daughter entered the marriage.

It is understandable, too, that where young people have grown up in a generous and loving home, they should want not to hurt their parents but rather to please them and make them happy. It is important, however, that young people make their own choices and that they make their own marriage and family decisions after marriage.

It is more difficult for some parents to learn to respect the personalities of their children and their freedom to make their own choices. And in learning to make their crucial life decisions many young people can well profit from the counsel and experience and perspective of older people. But it is hard to accept

the advice of those who are close to you and who are
emotionally involved.

For this reason, talking your marriage problems
over with a teacher or social worker, a friend, marriage
counselor, or clergyman is important. Young people
are often in revolt against certain elements in their
background or experience that distort their perspective. They cannot easily see the kinds of experience
they may encounter in the future, even though these
experiences may test their relationship to the breaking
point.

Thus we have seen that the pressures of families
and friends as well as of churches are often thrown
against religious intermarriage. Indeed, a religious intermarriage calls for an adjustment by parents and by
friends that many find hard to make. The probability
that their young people will achieve a happy marriage
is much greater when they do make such an adjustment successfully.

Where parents have kept a child close or dependent
in earlier years, a mixed marriage may be hazardous
unless the young person has made considerable progress
in learning to stand on his own feet and is ready to
make basic decisions with his mate.

Where the feelings of the parents on religion are
intense and dogmatic, it is important that the young
person know his own mind and take the responsibility
that is his regarding his own life. In matters of religion as well as in other matters, a husband and wife
should stand by one another and give one another
security and backing when it comes to conflict with
in-laws.

Sometimes parental domination is evident early and must be dealt with early. The marriage ceremony is not as important as the marriage itself. Yet the working out of the details concerning the wedding may be crucially important in determining the future relations with in-laws.

It is the young people who are being married. On all important matters their wishes should prevail. Compromise is justified in details and unimportant matters provided there is firmness on the important ones.

But if the wedding arrangements raise a doubt concerning the son's or daughter's emancipation from parental controls, then it may be necessary to stand firm on the issues revolving around the wedding ceremony in order to lay a sound basis from the very beginning for the relations of the couple with the family.

The Matter of Friends

Friends are important to the happiness of a family and a home. Every married pair wants to have some people who are congenial and close and who form a cluster of families that make up their intimate circle of friends. Sometimes "friends" fall away when one enters a mixed marriage.

Both in family and friendship a mixed marriage may face special hazards in a small community or in a community that is of one religious belief. Many couples have found that they are rejected by both religious groups from which they have come, Catholic and non-Catholic, Christian and Jewish, Judeo-Christian and Eastern.

In such a case, it takes strong character and a firm

bond of love, as well as friendliness and a spirit of service to others, to live in a community where one is well known. It may be necessary, in fact, to move to a city in which there are large sections of liberal opinion and numbers of families who can form a community of friends and lend support to those who dare to form interreligious unions.

The answer lies within the couple themselves. And here much depends upon whether they were attracted to one another and crossed the lines of traditional religious division out of weakness and desire for escape from their kind. Or whether they crossed the line because they were secure and strong and ready to reach out for broader contacts and richer living with those of different viewpoint and gifts and rhythms and religious views.

What of the Children?

Children present the greatest challenge to those who enter mixed marriages. The problem is a real one. It has two major aspects that must be carefully considered.

First, the psychological welfare of a child, his emotional and mental health, are fundamentally dependent upon the security of the home, the strength of the marriage, and the ways in which the parents work together for the child's welfare. Religious differences need not be a problem. In fact, they may even enrich a home if they add to its security and strengthen the common spiritual values for which it stands.

For it is not really the religious differences themselves but the way the husband and wife, the mother and father, see their differences that matters. Whether beliefs are the same or different, the kind of religion that means living in understanding and love helps to create a climate in the home that makes for emotional and mental health. If, however, the parents are in conflict over religion, or feel guilty at having married outside their faith, the religious factor can play havoc with the welfare of the children.

✓ Second, the religious training of the children can become ground for conflict and division. This is no simple matter unless both parents eventually embrace the same faith. It may afford little trouble if both partners agree to a broad and liberal interfaith training. This might include the history of religions and stress an attitude of reverence, the worth of the individual, and the supreme importance of moral values common to all faiths.

Here again, the way in which man and wife approach their differences is all important. If there is confidence and trust in one another; if there is a desire to work the problem out together; if there is clarity on those values that come first, then whatever the religious backgrounds, the religious education of the children can be worked out without becoming a source of unhappiness.

There may be only one church in the community. There may be no church or religious group at all with a program suitable to meet the needs of the children as this man and wife conceive them. Whatever the difficulties, the married pair can work them out only if they themselves are sound in their marriage relationship. And they will find the task much easier if they have a common ground in belief and practices and have developed their own family rituals to bind them more closely together.

When a marriage is childless and the couple desire children through adoption, great care has to be exercised in approaching adoption agencies. (In many communities children are available for foster care and adoption only if the children are placed with families of the same religion as that of the natural mother of the child. Where the law requires this, or where the practice of child placement agencies is sectarian placement, the couple of mixed religious background find it extremely difficult to obtain a child.)

Fortunately, a few agencies put their chief emphasis on whether the couple are happily married, love children, have a good home, and would make excellent parents.

How It Adds Up

The religious factor in marriage is only one among many. Misunderstanding and conflict between man and wife is not limited by any means to the religious factor where the partners are of different traditions and beliefs. Even within the same faith, whether it be a Catholic, a Protestant, or a Jewish marriage, the relationships may vary from happiness to a merely tolerable marriage and finally even to great unhappiness and possibly separation.

Differences in religious affiliation and belief may

or may not affect the happiness of a marriage. As with other differences, much depends on how important they are in the minds of the married pair. Where these interests are not very strong or where the couple are united in a basic religious outlook or where their love is stronger than traditional loyalties, then differences in belief or affiliation need not cause serious difficulty.

Religious intermarriage can be a mistake if the sectarian aspects of religious beliefs of the husband and wife are stronger than their love. These forces can pull that love apart.

If one member is devoutly religious and the other is weak in religious interest or is non-religious, and if the devout member holds a strongly dogmatic faith, it is difficult to see how the marriage can avoid conflict. Even if the non-religious person is willing to yield on all matters, it is difficult to see how there can be a sound basis for growing love and unity.

For one partner would be trying to bring the other to acceptance and outward conformity; that is, trying to impose religion because it is so important to him. The other is accepting that imposition because it seems unimportant. Only a very strong love and many common interests could give stability to such a marriage.

If there are important religious differences, a couple should have other strong bonds to make their marriage effective and happy. There would have to be a security in one another far beyond legal obligation. There would have to be a strong bond of love, genuine concern for one another, and many common interests. Beyond these, each would have to be secure in his own faith and know the other's faith and genuinely respect it.

In such a marriage there could be no secret thought that "Thank God, I was born in my faith and not in his. Though I may say that all faiths are equal, I know in my heart of hearts that they aren't. I shall pray for him and convert him and save him despite himself."

The difficulty in such a case is that the more one partner holds his own faith to be the one true faith, the less he can genuinely respect his partner's faith. And unless there is this recognition of the truth and value in the other's faith, how can there be equality in the relation of husband and wife? Or a sound basis for the rearing and religious training of children?

Indeed, not only must there be an equality of faiths, but also there must be, before marriage, a thorough discussion and meeting of minds and hearts on such matters as religious observance, dietary rules, money contributions, the religious education of children, and the role of the religious ideas of families and clergy.

Only by knowing one another thoroughly before marriage, only by testing one another's values and seeing each other's religious life as it works out in the families of both partners, can there be enough knowledge to give assurance that religious differences will not break the marriage. It may be possible to make adjustment through discussion and compromises. But it is better to know beforehand what the real difficulties are and to withdraw from the marriage venture, if need be, than to enter romantically a relationship that may bring only misery and conflict in the end.

Value of Guidance

It is because young men and women in love see one another with emotional hungers and passions, it is because romance blurs the sight and love makes so many things seem far simpler than they are, that it is good to have help in facing the realities of marriage. All young people engaged to be married should seek guidance in their problems.

Marriage is a choice made in freedom. Marriage is the beginning of a family and home in which two lives are joined to create something new and fresh and different. But the counselor can point out difficulties, can indicate implications, can share lessons out of past experience, and so can help the individual make his decisions with greater awareness of what is involved and with greater wisdom and maturity.

Difficulties can be overcome and have been overcome in many instances. Even if both partners start from different traditions and beliefs and associations, they can transcend these if their love is central and strong enough. Whether they attend separate churches or join the same religious fellowship or work out their religious life within the family without any affiliation, the important thing is the way of life the husband and wife experience day by day in the home.

Intermarriage between young people of different religious ancestry and tradition may lead to many positive values if both parties are tolerant in religious outlook. Concern for one another's welfare and for the children, a sharing of common interests, a basic agreement on the importance of things—these are the strands of life that bind lives together in devotion and unity.

Where love makes for such a marriage, the diverse religious backgrounds may enrich the common life.

In such a marriage the issues of religious belief, church attendance, the religious training of children, the use of birth control, relations with in-laws, can fall into their proper perspective. Indeed, the very challenge of these problems and the effort to work them out together may make for a dynamic factor in the marriage itself and may bring the family and home life to an even greater richness and maturity, a deeper love, and a stronger faith.

Such a marriage can mean enlarged horizons. It has implications for better intergroup relations and unity in the democratic community, and may even contribute indirectly toward greater international understanding.

CHAPTER 7

Let's Talk Sense About Sex!

By LESTER A. KIRKENDALL with ELIZABETH OGG

SUPPOSE our society's attitudes toward automobile driving were like its attitudes toward sex.

Except for jokes and oblique allusions, we'd shun the subject. While privately debating when and how to explain it to teenagers, we'd try to keep them out of the driver's seat. Driver training in the schools would arouse some hysterical protests. The rising toll of auto accidents would be greeted by laments about a breakdown in morals, instead of research to find out why people killed and maimed one another on the highways.

And all the while, countless books, magazines, movies, and advertisements would glamorize the thrills of driving—with or without a license!

After providing all kinds of opportunities for youth to learn to drive, we are in fact quite lenient with young traffic offenders. But after giving youth only partial or confused sexual instruction, along with

From "Sex and Our Society," Public Affairs Pamphlet No. 366

much popular glamorization of sex, we roundly condemn those who have sexual relations before they
marry.

Does this make sense?

At last such questions are being publicly asked. A
fresh, objective look at human sexual needs in the
light of present conditions is being urged not only
by professionals who deal with sexual matters, but also
by ministers, educators, lawyers, writers, and editors.
If we cannot arrive at more sensible and realistic sexual standards, they feel, matters will get worse. We
shall lose the chance to govern the course of the
changes that are taking place, whether we like them or
not.

What Is "Right"?

Not all western societies agree on acceptable sexual
behavior. Some consider a full sexual relation with
one person before marriage immoral, but see no harm
in petting many different partners. Others sanction intercourse for engaged couples, but frown on casual
petting as promiscuous, vulgar, and frustrating. Cultural attitudes toward extramarital affairs also run a
wide gamut, from condoning to condemning.

This diversity of cultural patterns contributes new
uncertainties to the sexual thinking of our people,
young and old, since today no culture can insulate itself from others. From anthropologists we learn of
societies we thought less advanced than ours that
seem to have healthier attitudes toward sex. Americans
traveling abroad by the thousands, and foreigners

visiting the United States, have prompted cultural comparisons.

Even stay-at-homes see these differences through movies, TV, and newspapers. Hence none of us can be sure that our traditional sex code is "right." Young people certainly do not accept it without question.

With our values in flux, everyone becomes his own moralist. Even those who cling to the traditional standards, as many still do, seldom criticize others who claim sexual freedom. A person's sex code, they feel, is something he has to decide for himself.

In a college sophomore's words, "There is good love and bad love and just because you happen to be married is no guarantee of either."

For many, sex relations are the ultimate form of communion between a man and a woman who are deeply committed to each other. Some may feel justified in consummating such a relationship without being legally wed. For others, sexual intercourse is no more than a pastime, or perhaps an act of rebellion, for which any tolerable partner will do.

A young woman may accept a man's advances in the hope of pushing him toward marriage, while another has sex relations out of blind hunger for affection. In twos and threes, some teenage boys spur each other on to intercourse with prostitutes or pickups. They boast of their exploits in their male group in order to win the status of "men." But other adolescents, drawn unintentionally into sex relations through petting, worry about their conduct.

Despite the social sanction marriage enjoys, much

unhappiness can stem from the denial or the twisted expression of sex by husband or wife. One spouse may use it to manipulate the other, to belittle or to punish. In the later years, frank enjoyment of sex is generally deprecated.)

Clearly, human sex is not one kind of experience, but many—uplifting or degrading, tender or cruel, fulfilling or frustrating. When sex "goes wrong," people get hurt—and these include not only the desperate young women who seek illegal abortions or rush into unhappy marriages, or the unwed mothers and their children. Others also are harmed, sometimes more deeply, by the practice of deceit and exploitation, by anxiety and guilt, by the stunting of their personal growth and of their capacity for genuine relationships.

Talk About It!

Both teenage boys and girls rate "petting" and "sex" as more difficult to discuss with their parents than any other of thirty-six topics, according to one study. According to another, adults don't even support the sexual conduct of which they approve. For example, virgin boys complain that, while boys their own age put them on the defensive about their chastity, their elders give them no encouragement in maintaining it.

As a rule, adults have no idea what pattern of sexual conduct their sons and daughters are following unless something goes wrong. Then they react with shock, blind to the fact that the basic failure is their own—a reflection of our social confusion.

There is need to discuss openly how different patterns of sexual behavior serve human beings. If young people must decide for themselves what they will do, they should know where their decisions are likely to lead.

Some sort of early warning system to head off destructive sexual experiences would seem to be common sense. But here our society has fallen down badly. Except for receiving depersonalized accounts of the physiology of sex and generalized exhortations that have little pertinence to their daily lives, the young have been pretty much left to find their own answers in this field.

To speak frankly of sex and admit its pleasures, some grown-ups fear, would be to "open the floodgates" to sexual license.

But do we expect every one to go on an eating rampage when we pay attention to food, and learn how to make it nutritious as well as tasty and attractive? Those who overeat are driven not by physical but by psychological hunger. And when their emotional needs are met in healthy ways, they can more easily manage their appetite. The same holds true for the sexual appetite.

It is time to overcome the inhibitions that distort our view of our society's sexual problems, and to try to deal with these problems rationally. The best way to begin is with an honest, open discussion. Neither blasé attitudes toward sex nor over-simple straitlaced prohibitions are adequate for today.

The Results of Changes

Today we have not one but several American sex codes, varying by region, religion, age, and social-economic group. Whether we approve them or not, they represent attempts to chart a course in a time of rapid and bewildering change.

We are all familiar with the physical aspects of this change—the new technology, with its jet planes, automation, and vast urban complexes; the medical advances that have lengthened the life span; the explosion of population; space science. But many of us are unprepared for the accompanying revolution in thinking and behavior.

When the emancipated woman came in and the chaperone went out, some of the old sexual restraints were bound to give way. This was even more inevitable since the automobile, the bachelor apartment, and—more recently—the motel, offered ample opportunities for privacy and anonymity.

In addition, earlier puberty and a longer life span have extended potential sex life, and the new leisure gives most people more time and energy to take advantage of it. This is particularly true of women. Released from the burdens of excessive childbearing, they need no longer fear sex. In middle age they are not too worn out to have zest for it.

Sex Without "Consequences"

Modern contraceptives, which have made it possible to separate sex from procreation, exert a powerful pressure for change. Swiftly escalating populations, in our own as well as underdeveloped lands, offer mankind only two alternatives: to wait for war, famine, or disease to put a brake on runaway population growth, or to curb the birth rate. Curbing the birth rate means either separating sex from reproduction or largely abstaining from sexual intercourse.

But to restrict expression of human sexuality to the needs of population growth today would be to deny men and women normal sexual outlets for the greater part of their lives. Few people would accept such a restriction—as indeed few do now.

Many religious leaders are now sanctioning birth control for wedded couples. It is in fact equally available to single men and women today. Drugstores in forty-eight of the fifty states sell contraceptives of various kinds without prescription. Younger adolescents who might not be able to buy them can often obtain them from older or more experienced friends.

Some teenagers, it is true, hesitate to take any precaution against pregnancy, since making intercourse a planned act destroys a typical defense against guilt— "We didn't mean to, but we were carried away." Others, particularly among the college group, pride themselves on contraceptive know-how, although they may be erratic in applying it. If they feel guilt, they find other ways of rationalizing it.

Down With Repression!

Freud's exposé of the harm done by Victorian sexual repressions—or rather, the popular interpretation of Freud's findings—seems to sanction sexual freedom. In this view, sex relations become the royal road to health. For women, at least, they are also proof of "ability to give."

Perhaps the kind of upbringing today's teenagers have had predisposes them to fall in with this view. Their parents, after all, grew up in difficult depression days and were determined to give their children an easier and better life if they possibly could. Some middle-class parents who made good on this determination also tended to be permissive, because their child-rearing "bibles" seemed to urge this.

Emphasis on rigorous discipline and duty gave way to approval of *enjoyment* as an end in itself. As a result, a whole generation has grown up long on freedom to seek pleasure, but short on ability to postpone it until they can harmonize it with longer-term goals.

The affluent society has abetted this trend. In an economy of abundance that relies on constantly increasing consumption, the old virtues of hard work, self-denial, and saving for the future seem less valid. Daily pressure to buy on impulse and have fun— "Why wait? Buy now, pay later"—encourages self-indulgence. And a myriad stimuli prompt indulgence in sexual pleasures.

Here is the deadly core of our cultural contradictions. We are said to be moving from sex-denial to sex-affirmation, but it is a devious move. We do not affirm sex as a healthy human drive to be harmonized with other healthy human drives. Our culture insidiously presents it as a stolen sweet, a commercial asset, fun, a weapon, a status symbol, a cure for loneliness and, above all, the crowning expression of romantic love.

But our culture still officially labels it *sin*—outside the bonds of matrimony.

Adults as well as youth are snared in the contradiction. Since so many adults violate the traditional code, it is not surprising that their lip service to it does not persuade the young to do better. On the contrary, adolescents see social authority as two-faced and consequently are apt to flout its rules.

If traditional morality no longer serves as a curb, neither does fear of consequences. The partisans of sexual freedom still worry about possible pregnancy, venereal disease, and community censure, of course. But in our era of contraceptives, penicillin, and relative parental leniency, these are no longer absolute tragedies.

Indeed, the rising incidence of VD among teenagers and of out-of-wedlock pregnancies at various age and social-economic levels show how little deterrent power these once-dreaded consequences have.

What About "Chastity"?

All these trends toward a more carefree, hedonistic sexual expression have certainly not swept the old conventions away entirely. Most teenagers still believe in waiting for sexual fulfillment until they marry, and many people, of all ages, are faithful to their marriage partners.

But those who are chaste are increasingly pressed to defend their stand, especially by those who ridicule virginity as a sign of immaturity.

The word "chastity" itself is subject to new interpretations. For some adolescent girls it means, not old-fashioned "purity," but simply the preservation of an intact hymen through a gamut of sex play that includes "everything but—." Some play the game with more than one partner, in a new kind of promiscuity that enables the girl to remain technically a "virgin." Others limit it to a steady or fiancé.

Both techniques are attempts to cope with the contradictions in our cultural attitudes toward sex. So are many youthful marriages.

Before entering a sweeping condemnation of these diverse modes of sexual expression, ought we not to consider them dispassionately? After all, not being a virgin does not, in itself, make a young woman a tramp. And we might ask whether strict premarital chastity *always* furthers personal growth. It may stem from fear of sex, which also can lead to unhappiness in marriage. We need a stronger moral base than that.

The Single Standard?

Relations between the sexes are more democratic today. Men and women are expected to understand and respect one another. And women are expected to enjoy sex, not just endure it. Though far from fully accepted, this ideal has already shaken the double standard.

Insofar as it moves the sexes toward equal status, this new democracy represents a gain. But what should a single standard be?

Where one exists, as it does among a growing number of college boys and girls, it may prescribe premarital chastity for both, sex with affection for both, or casual sex for both. Dr. Ira Reiss, who wrote *Premarital Sex Standards in America*, believes that the second will ultimately become the predominant American pattern.

But in moving toward a single sexual standard, we cannot altogether ignore biological realities. Men will probably always be more interested in the sex act, and women in what goes before and after—in the whole climate of the relationship. Since in sex a woman risks a much greater involvement of herself and her body, her response is more nearly total and tends to draw her into deeper commitment, while sexual release frees a man to turn to other things.

Each must learn to appreciate and make allowance for the other's unavoidably different approach.

The Scientific Attitude

The quest for rational answers to all questions, which has been fostered by modern science, no longer stops short of the sexual area. Sex research has expanded to include studies of premarital sex, promiscuity, illegitimacy, homosexuality, sexual offenses, and sex in the later years, with emphasis on the motives behind the different modes of sexual expression. It has already demolished some taboos.

Today children are rarely threatened with sterility or madness if they masturbate, for example. It is now known that the practice is almost universal and does no physical harm. Parents are advised to take a relaxed view of it, unless it interferes with a child's other normal activities.

In addition, fewer people nowadays feel that infidelity makes a divorce imperative. Extramarital affairs are in fact far more prevalent than divorces. They are not always an expression of boredom, frustration, or self-indulgence.

Those "triangles" in which all three participants are sensitively concerned to avoid hurting others are rarely reported or dramatized. Such affairs do, of course, almost always hurt someone. But therapists can cite cases in which the wife's learning of her husband's love affair (or vice versa) has forced the partners to face the problems in their marriage. This often has reopened clogged communications, eventually leading to a new lease on life for the marriage.

As sex research has expanded, its findings have been reported in popular reading matter. Freedom to discuss sex in the mass media has grown appreciably. This, too, helps to create a climate for forthright discussion of sex.

And candor is slowly making its way into the schools. Some high school biology books still stop short of the subject of human reproduction, or give it only a few obscure lines. But in the last few years texts that do cover this important subject have been prepared under the auspices of the Biological Sciences Curriculum Study and have been introduced into a number of schools, both public and parochial. It is encouraging to note that most of the parents whose children are using these texts have wholeheartedly endorsed this move.

Most candid of all are the young, both among themselves and with professional adults who meet them on their own level and do not sit in judgment on them. Young people's ability to talk honestly about sex far exceeds that of most parents and teachers, and their conversation is based on their own experiences. Although these often reflect rebellion and confusion, selfishness and irresponsibility, they also reveal idealism and tenderness, and a search for identity and relationship.

Sex and the Whole Human Being

A key question for science is, How does sexual behavior relate to human personality as a whole? Results of several studies confirm what common sense might have told us, if we hadn't wrenched sex out of context: namely, that the sex drive does not function independently of other human drives.

As modern psychosomatic medicine has shown, the performance of the various bodily organs is not determined by a local condition alone, but by the total interaction of body, mind, and environment. So, too, sex is a function neither of the sex organs alone, nor of the body alone, but of the whole human being in relation to his world.

Sexual impulses are basic and powerful, of course, but a human being has other impulses, too—to win social approval and love, to serve, to achieve, to satisfy curiosity, to make money, to gain power or prestige, sometimes to take revenge, perhaps to fail. In a given situation one or more of these and other motives may temper, reinforce, or even cancel out the sex drive.

Interviews reveal that promiscuous people, whether adolescent or adult, turn to sex less for physical gratification than in an effort to relieve emotional tensions and to gain satisfactions that they have been unable to find in other ways. Many come from backgrounds filled with conflict, rejection, failure, and emotional deprivation.

A 20-year-old college girl whom we'll call Sally is a good example. She has had intercourse with several men, whose initial advances she promptly accepted. She has now become an avid sex-seeker herself because, she says, "I like it when they love me."

As a child of well-to-do parents, Sally was reared by a series of maids. Everything that money could buy was hers, at her whim—but not love.

Then, when she was in her late teens, the family fortunes collapsed. Totally unequipped to earn a living, yet pressured by her parents to do so, she felt grossly betrayed. Her parents hate her, she says. Judging by their public remarks about her "worthless" and "spoiled-childish ingratitude," she isn't far wrong.

Emotionally deprived herself, Sally has no love to give. Yet in her desperate need to feel wanted and to belong somewhere, she welcomes each sexual advance. Through sex relations she seems to be grasping for the illusory sensation of being loved.

Studies of prostitutes and pick-ups have uncovered similar patterns of unhappy, often disorganized family life and attempts to meet the resulting emotional problems through promiscuity.

An "Oversexed" Young Man

It is much the same with men. From age 15 on, John, now 20, has associated with pick-ups and prostitutes. He thinks he is "oversexed." Yet he admits that he gets little satisfaction out of his sexual exploits.

John comes of a respectable but cold family. A dominating mother has stifled his initiative by means of tight controls. He fears rather than loves her. His father, a successful professional man, has offered him little but biting criticisms.

Despite his intelligent mind, John has been a mediocre student and hasn't distinguished himself in any way. His college career is a failure. He expects to be dropped from college any day now, and sees no future except "to go into the service."

Can you wonder that John never feels accepted? He dates a girl occasionally, but seldom manages to get a second date, and never a third. Recently he realized that he resents women and takes a perverse pleasure in "loving them and leaving them." For him, sex is mainly an effort to discharge his bitterness

—his rage against his parents and his despair about himself.

"No Future"

This feeling of hopelessness, of having no aim or direction, turned up frequently among teenagers in New York City venereal disease clinics. The young people were studied by Dr. Celia Deschin.

The majority of the 600 teenage boys and girls interviewed came from low-income, but for the most part decent, families in which the parents did try to set standards. Their most common problems were school failure, truancy, dropping out of school, joblessness, and a general feeling that they had nothing to do.

As Dr. Deschin points out, "Having nothing to do—in the sense of having few meaningful and socially useful responsibilities—means essentially to *be* nothing." Lacking a role and purpose, such young people are more prone to turn to casual sex in a spirit of "Why not? What else is there?"

Where the pattern persists in adult life, researchers have found no evidence of greater-than-average sexuality, but rather personality disturbances and a lack of capacity for sustained affection.

Of course, such findings do not prove that every one who has been spared an unfavorable upbringing or cultural deprivation will be sexually temperate. But since adverse emotional influences can distort the sex drive, it seems likely that positive ones can help to give it mature direction.

Dr. Martin Loeb studied "good" teenagers to learn what distinguished them from those who contracted and spread venereal disease. (Adolescents least apt to be drawn into irresponsible sex, he tentatively concluded, are those who respect themselves, believe they can contribute to others and can rely on them, and feel at ease in their sex roles—"the boys like being boys and want to be men, and the girls like being girls and want to be women.")

But the study also revealed how hard it is for teenagers to develop self-respect when adults overprotect or constantly criticize them. "Adults behave as if they thought of adolescents as childish, irresponsible, and dangerous," many youngsters said. Even the "good" teenagers felt that such a rating justified the "bad" ones in living up to it.

Sex Without Relationship

Another way of tracing differences between responsible and irresponsible sexual behavior is to examine the relationships of the participants. This is what one of the authors (Kirkendall) did in an inquiry into the premarital sex experiences of college men.

In liaisons devoid of real relationships, such as those with prostitutes, pick-ups, or young women whom the men dated with sex alone in mind, there was almost no intellectual or emotional exchange. There was also no concern for the woman's feelings, nor any effort to protect her from harm such as pregnancy, publicity, or feelings of guilt or humiliation.

Typical of the lack of communication was this statement:

"We never talked about intercourse, either before or after . . . When we quit going together we still said nothing, though I think she got to thinking I was using her. At any rate she became more and more unwilling for intercourse. I still see her sometimes, but we do little more than nod as we pass."

Most young men secured their physical pleasure at the expense of feelings of dissatisfaction, even disgust, on other counts—"I felt kinda cheap afterwards," as one said.

In their pursuit of sex, the young men used deceitful persuasive tactics and even downright threats on their dates. For example:

"I told her I loved her, and all that baloney."

"I said I knew about her sexual relationship with my buddy, and if she didn't come across everyone in school would know about it."

Nor was the exploitation all on one side. A young woman might use her sex in an attempt to ensnare the man:

"I sorta realized that I was taking advantage of her and that made me feel a little guilty. But she was taking advantage, too. She was pushing all the time to get me to say I was interested in marriage. I never agreed or disagreed with her marriage talk. I just listened and went along for the sex, but all the time I was respecting her less."

Sex With Affection

But where affection had flowered before sexual desire, and especially when a couple were engaged, physical intimacy more often expressed emotional closeness, Professor Kirkendall found. In many more of these situations the partners first discussed whether or not to "go all the way," and, if they did, experienced an even greater flow of understanding talk afterwards.

Each was concerned for the other and for the future of the relationship, and took responsibility for protecting the other's well-being and good name.

Some couples who experimented with sex were disturbed by it. One young man felt that he and his fiancée had drawn much closer, not through coitus itself, but because the experience "shook us up so that we had to talk it through, and we came to a real understanding." They decided to forego sex relations until marriage.

While admitting to some fear of pregnancy or guilt at breaking with parental values, other couples believed that intercourse had enhanced their relationship and helped them to talk more openly together. Several married couples said that it had allowed them to solve problems of sexual adjustment before the wedding.

Not all engaged couples were so positive, however. A few young men had obviously used an engagement to cloak the selfish pursuit of sex. A man might promise, "If you get pregnant, we'll get married right away," yet be unaware of the responsibilities involved and be unready to cope with them.

Some had mistaken sexual passion for love. Under the pressure society puts upon them to marry, women were apt, on the flimsiest grounds, to believe it was love. Such associations soon broke up. "We were too immature. We just got in over our heads," was a typical comment.

An Enduring Attachment

Could these young people have known whether intercourse would strengthen or weaken their relationship? Obviously they couldn't. Premarital sex is like driving a car at high speed: You can know the outcome only after you've covered the course.

But you *can* know something about testing the quality of a relationship.

Essential for building a sound one is time. It takes more than a few days or weeks to achieve full, honest communication, mutual understanding and trust. Relationships less than six months old more often fell apart after embarking on sex than did older ones, the Kirkendall study found.

The hasty couples had apparently thrust upon their budding friendship the strain of a complex experience it was not yet strong enough to bear. At deeper levels of attachment, concern for the relationship is a more important consideration for the couple than desire for physical pleasure.

Another essential is mutual respect. This leaves each partner free to decide how far he or she, with their differing concerns, wants to go in the relationship, without the other cajoling in an effort to force the pace.

Still another sign of health is openness to the world

around them. As St. Exupéry said, "Love does not consist in gazing into each other's eyes, but in looking out together in the same direction." If neither partner cares to join the other in activities reaching beyond their personal encounter, their liaison is a dead-end street. But where a couple steadily enlarge their human sympathies and are themselves accepted by more and more people, their relationship becomes a bridge to a wider world.

In any event, no two people can so completely isolate themselves that what they do will have no implications for the rest of society. As social beings, they must consider the possible effects of their decisions on others as well as themselves.

This does not mean invariably conforming to the wishes of others, but carefully weighing opposing needs and views. At times it is necessary to stand on principles that run counter to common practice, because to do so promises more freedom for oneself and others to grow. Such an independent stand takes courage, for it may disturb existing relationships with family and friends.

No Rule Fits All Cases

In the light of these considerations, the question of whether to condemn or condone premarital intercourse fades into the background. It is not the act or its timing on which we should focus, but its motive and circumstances.

If we value sexuality as a part of our human endowment, along with intelligence, physique, aptitudes, talents, and so on, then we may ask: How can we use all our gifts to develop genuine personal relationships that will enrich our lives?

And, if we agree that personal relationships are the central issue, the improvement of such relations can serve as a basis for building a life-affirming moral code. Our key criteria then might be:

MORAL BEHAVIOR leads to:	IMMORAL BEHAVIOR leads to:
Integrity in relationships	Duplicity in relationships
Trust of others	Distrust of others
Broadening of human sympathies	Barriers between persons and between groups
Cooperative attitudes	Uncooperative, hostile attitudes
Enhanced self-respect	
Consideration for others' rights and needs	Diminished self-respect
	Exploitation of others
Individual fulfillment and zest for living	Stunting of individual growth and disillusionment

Judged by these criteria, most of the nonmarital and some of the marital sex in America today would have to be called immoral, because it is exploitive and unfulfilling.

Even with a genuine effort to follow a moral course in these terms, some people would make mistakes. But a mistake can be a learning experience, and the penalties could be less harsh than they often are in our present condition of chaos.

After an investment of time sufficient to develop free, honest communication, a couple can often clarify their feelings and motives. If they find that these are not compatible, they can perhaps part without becoming sexually involved, and without too much pain. But if they do experiment with sex only to have their relationship founder, their honest effort to understand and be responsible to one another may well have been more gain than loss.

Even the pain of parting—and it will be deeper in proportion to the time and emotion invested in the relationship—can then be a potential for growth. Many therapists have seen such an experience lead to greater maturity.

In the Long Run?

Does premarital intercourse benefit or hamper later marriage relations? It's hard to say, since so many other factors—personality, upbringing, surrounding social attitudes—are involved.

From the viewpoint of married couples themselves, the effects range all the way from strengthening to damaging. Men and women who have grown up with relatively few inhibitions about sex are, on the whole, less likely to suffer than those who were strictly taught. Before attributing marital troubles to the mere fact that the partners had premarital sexual experiences, therefore, we should consider the partners' personalities and the cultural influences that may have made the experiences a source of shame.

The *kind* of premarital sex, whether casual or caring, will also have a bearing on the outcome.

With the sanction of his male group, many a man learns to take sex wherever he can get it, with no thought for his partners. Some claim that such experiences have helped their sexual adjustment in marriage. Maybe on the purely physical side they have.

Yet promiscuity usually involves deceit, social irresponsibility, and taking advantage. It divorces sex from personality and empties it of tenderness.

The basic attitudes that lead some men to adopt this pattern *before* marriage may underlie their failures *after* marriage. As one man who was in marital difficulties put it, "My wife says that I treat her like a girl in the back seat of a car." And he admitted that she was right.

Some promiscuous young women express confidence that they will be faithful and devoted wives, but too few have been followed up in marriage to test this belief.

It's Up to Adults!

To arrive at a rational sexual code, we must first get the problem in proper focus—as an *adult* problem. True, one of youth's tasks is to integrate sex into their lives. But the fact that many fail to do so is largely due to *the lack of adult help*. First and foremost, adults need sex education.

Both teenage boys and girls have, in research interviews, expressed a wish to discuss sexual questions with adults whom they can trust and who will not scold. Such adults, it seems, are more apt to be found outside the family than within it.

First, Accept Sexuality

If adults could all view sexual arousal and learning how to manage it as a normal part of growing up, they might shed irrational fears and be able to talk about it straightforwardly. Many people can't do this because they have never worked through their own sexual problems.

A mother who still feels guilt over masturbation, for example, cannot discuss it freely with her children. And a father who has never come to terms with his own premarital affairs may be in an awkward spot when his son inquires, "Dad, did you have intercourse before you were married?"

One 17-year-old boy who reported such a confrontation added, "He swallowed, got red in the face and said, 'Yes.' That's the last word I heard."

Still, even liberated parents sometimes betray anxiety in talking of sex with their children, who then sense something "bad" about it. With teenagers, the problem becomes even more difficult. At this age youngsters insist on thinking their own thoughts and going their own way without parents "butting in." It is part of their striving for independence.

In many cases, the parents' wisest course is to accept the fact that an outside person may be better able to help their son or daughter in this phase, and to see that such a helper is available.

Open Communications

Adults who accept their own sexuality and remember the sweetness, the strangeness, and bewilderment of its burgeoning will not demand that adolescents deny all sexual feelings, but will help them understand how to manage these feelings harmlessly.

Our culture with its present attitudes certainly hedges nonmarital sex about with hazards, and for many young people such experiences work out unsatisfactorily. But in their concern with this problem, adults must not behave as if they wanted to deny youth the right to ultimate full sexual experience. They must help them achieve it in a rewarding way, without endangering their own or others' welfare.

To this end, adolescents should have full, frank answers to all their questions about sex. As parents give their children freedom, they must also give them knowledge, so that they can use their freedom intelligently and responsibly.

To say that this will "push them into sex" is to ignore reality. They are pushed into sex already, and some of the most damaging consequences are due to half-truths youth have been handed, or to sheer ignorance. An example of this is the pregnant teenager who had learned only that "such things didn't happen to girls of good family like herself."

If adults give youngsters biological instruction without at the same time making restraints an issue, they may be surprised to find adolescents themselves coming around to this question. Teenagers are interested in more than mere physical satisfactions, as adults who work with them know. They want to understand sex in its psychological as well as physical dimensions.

Relax Tensions

Opening up an honest dialogue and relaxing tensions surrounding the subject of sex would in themselves alleviate certain sexual problems. For instance, children's encounters with indecent exposure would do them little harm if grown-ups did not get so agitated about them. Unless others convey alarm, a child is more likely to be curious than to be disturbed about a public display of genital organs.

Similarly, sexual play between young boys would generally have little effect on their future sexual patterns if adults who learned of it could see it as a normal phase of development. Fewer young men would then be driven into life-long homosexuality because horrified parents or teachers pinned the label on them when they were in their teens.

How people react to an out-of-wedlock affair can also affect the outcome. Dr. Harold Christensen's comparative studies of premarital sex and premarital pregnancies in Utah, Indiana, and Denmark have estimated the highest incidence of both in Denmark —usually at somewhat older ages than in this country. Yet the consequences for young Danes seems to be far less damaging than here, because the Danish culture is more willing to accept intercourse between partners who are engaged or going steady.

Hence guilt and conflict over premarital sex are minimal in Denmark, and partners faced with a pregnancy rarely rush into a shotgun wedding. They may even let the child be born before they marry, since there is little stigma on illegitimacy.

Even in our culture there is room for more than one kind of response to premarital pregnancies. Is it wise to insist on a shotgun marriage, for example? Forced, loveless, and immature as they often are, such marriages as often fail.

In the ones that succeed, the partners really care and have been backed by their families and often their church as well. The compassion of people who are important to them has helped them breast the crisis and continue to build their lives. The same can be true for a young woman who bears an illegitimate child.

Ease Pressures

Adults have a job to do, too, in combating the legacy left by our long history of using sex for ulterior ends. The age-old pressure of a woman to find a mate has even been stepped up in America of late.

As mothers' concern over their daughters' popularity rises, dating and marrying ages go down. With so short a period in which to compete, the race now begins in junior high school.

The pressures on a young man are somewhat different. "Many older men feel that boys are not men until they have had sexual intercourse," an adolescent complains. The physical act becomes a false gauge of maturity, a masculine status symbol.

Where the young woman wants a man, and the man wants sex, each is tempted to try to exploit the other. The woman offers sex in the hope of snaring the man, and the man aggressively seeks it to prove himself a man. The woman loses out, and the man finds real satisfaction eluding him like a will-o'-the-wisp.

(For it takes a mature man or woman, with feeling for others as well as a strong sense of self, to manage sex responsibly and at the same time enjoy it to the full.)

Stop False "Maturity"

There is confusion in our culture between the *process of growing up* and *being grown-up*, which by definition must come second. Growing up starts earlier now and is telescoped to such an extent that maturity is assumed long before it can be achieved.

If adults could see this more clearly, they would stop encouraging their children to play at grown-up life. They would think twice about subsidizing marriages for which the partners are not ready to be responsible. They would impress upon adolescents who do marry the desirability of postponing the birth of a child until they are more mature.

Youth need to test their capacities, of course. But nowadays young women might better be challenged to get an education before getting a man.

Asked why he went to Georgia to take part in civil rights demonstrations, a middle-class white boy replied, "As a test, to prove myself a man." More young men might be inspired to test their manhood through similar serious commitments, instead of through depersonalized sex.

No human society has held that the sex drive required no controls. But few have been as ambiguous and ostrich-like about it as ours.

Sex denied or pursued for selfish ends breeds emptiness and frustration, which can set the stage for aggression. It is time to lift our heads from the sand and use them—and our heart as well—to develop a healthy, constructive role for sexual energy throughout our lives.